SpringerBriefs in Criminology

SpringerBriefs in Criminology present concise summaries of cutting edge research across the fields of Criminology and Criminal Justice. It publishes small but impactful volumes of between 50-125 pages, with a clearly defined focus. The series covers a broad range of Criminology research from experimental design and methods, to brief reports and regional studies, to policy-related applications.

The scope of the series spans the whole field of Criminology and Criminal Justice, with an aim to be on the leading edge and continue to advance research. The series will be international and cross-disciplinary, including a broad array of topics, including juvenile delinquency, policing, crime prevention, terrorism research, crime and place, quantitative methods, experimental research in criminology, research design and analysis, forensic science, crime prevention, victimology, criminal justice systems, psychology of law, and explanations for criminal behavior.

SpringerBriefs in Criminology will be of interest to a broad range of researchers and practitioners working in Criminology and Criminal Justice Research and in related academic fields such as Sociology, Psychology, Public Health, Economics and Political Science.

More information about this series at http://www.springer.com/series/10159

Anna-Maria Getoš Kalac

Violence in the Balkans

First findings from the
Balkan Homicide Study

 Springer

Anna-Maria Getoš Kalac
University of Zagreb – Faculty of Law
Zagreb, Croatia

ISSN 2192-8533   ISSN 2192-8541   (electronic)
SpringerBriefs in Criminology
ISSN 2194-6213   ISSN 2194-6221 (electronic)
SpringerBriefs in Policing
ISBN 978-3-030-74493-9   ISBN 978-3-030-74494-6   (eBook)
https://doi.org/10.1007/978-3-030-74494-6

This Springer imprint is published by the registered company Springer Nature Switzerland AG
The registered company address is: Gewerbestrasse 11, 6330 Cham, Switzerland

Foreword

Criminological research on violence (and its causes) has a long history in Europe and continues to attract criminological attention. Lethal violence has become an important field of criminological research in Europe, not least visible in the 2012 *Handbook on European Homicide Research* and the 2014 *European Journal of Criminology Special Issue on Homicide*. However, these publications show clearly that research on lethal violence in the last decades is confined to only a handful of European countries with rather strong investments in criminology in general and a strong homicide research history in particular. Here, the book at hand *Violence in the Balkans. First Findings from the Balkan Homicide Study* first of all fills a knowledge gap in a region where the development of empirical criminology was delayed by significant obstacles after the Second World War and then in the 1990s as a consequence of the wars of secession. The book, though, demonstrates the growing capacity to carry out excellent criminological research and to advance homicide research in terms of theory adjusted to the particulars of the Balkan region. Although, the space available for this first publication is limited, the data collected offer a rich basis for further analysis and theorizing which may extend on various and sometimes politically sensitive issues which today mark the field of homicide research.

The book makes use of data drawn from case files, and as all Balkan countries belong to the family of civil law systems, this approach to homicide data collection is best suited to serve both leading goals of the study. Case files lend themselves to a description of lethal violence as detailed as possible on the one hand and to looking closely into the process of the normative definition and construction of homicide/murder on the other hand. At the center of the construction of a homicidal act lies the attribution of the intent to kill, and intent (and in addition various characteristics and motives of killing) serves as the very basis of parceling out those wrongs which should be eligible for the most serious criminal penalty available on criminal codes books. In Europe, after the abolition of the death penalty (except Belarus), social and normative construction of homicide takes place against the background of life imprisonment (or where life imprisonment is not on the criminal code book (like for example in Slovenia or Croatia), long prison sentences equaling essentially life imprisonment in other European countries which in many cases provide for parole from a life sentence after 15 to 20 years).

The history of homicide research in Europe shows the involvement of various disciplines. Among these, of course, forensic psychiatry and medicine were among those from which significant contributions may be noted, which is at least partially explained by the inquisitorial nature of criminal procedure codes requiring in-depth and full investigation (search for truth and a related interest of trial courts in avoiding successful appeals), in particular when it comes to the most serious crimes (and the most serious criminal penalties). While forensic psychiatry (guided by requests of criminal law and procedure) was focused most of the twentieth century on questions of whether and to what extent mental problems had impaired the cognitive capacity to discern right from wrong or the capacity to control an act, from the 1980s onward, security pursued by criminal law moved to the center of crime policies and forensic psychiatry was assigned the task of assessing and predicting dangerousness. Pursuit of security, moreover, started to trigger the question why in particular serial murder, school shootings, or other forms of excessive lethal violence were not prevented. This question, of course, is also carried by an interest of finding out who was responsible to prevent and who failed to comply with that responsibility.

Criminological research on violence, not only in Europe, traditionally has abstained from exploring wars, insurgencies, or terrorism. However, in particular, the Yugoslavian secession wars have raised interest in criminological circles to include genocide, war crimes, and crimes against humanity in the research agenda.

The book then reveals a picture of lethal violence which contrasts greatly with popular images of a violence-prone Balkan caused by a history of thriving banditry and a legacy of a weak state resulting from long-lasting foreign rule (as portrayed, for example, by German writer Karl May in the late nineteenth century). Though rates of lethal violence are somewhat higher in the Balkans than in the North, West, and the Center of Europe, compared to homicide rates observed in Eastern Europe, in the Americas, Africa, or parts of Asia, Balkan rates are much closer to their Western and Northern neighbors.

The book shows clearly that lethal violence in the Balkans is – as in the rest of Europe – today mostly intimate partner lethal violence. Homicidal acts are not carried out in the streets (and between strangers), they are rarely the result of conflicts in the underground economy and violent retaliation. Balkan countries are in general low-crime countries with urban centers today not exhibiting large-scale shadow economies, red-light districts, or open drug scenes. Even in times of flourishing shadow economies in the 1990s following political and economic transition and driven by civil war, the UNODC has noted for Southwestern Europe low and declining homicide rates. Homicides occur mostly within intimate relationships. This finding is most interesting as it shows that the almost complete disappearance of (male) stranger to (male) stranger homicides (though not the disappearance of war) and a corresponding sharp decline in European homicide rates during the last centuries observed by Manuel Eisner is not necessarily dependent on the emergence of a strong and effective monopoly of force held and maintained by a nation state modeled on European visions.

While it has been suggested that criminological research interests in Europe are increasingly emphasizing subgroups of homicides, placing the focus on certain subgroups (of victims or offenders) may also reflect political agendas, and not primarily scientific interest, and express the wish to find in criminal law a vehicle demonstrating the significance of agendas and the legitimate need for support. The ongoing debates on "femicide" and calls to introduce sentencing enhancements for femicide bear witness to an agenda which seeks particular consideration for victimization due to gender-related inequality, though the UNODC Global Study on Homicide notes for 2017 that globally 4 out of 5 victims of violent death are (young) men while 1 is female. But, UNODC at the same time points out that women are exposed to the heaviest burden of lethal violence (though small in numbers) which supposedly is caused by inequality and gender stereotypes. In fact, while today in Europe the risk of falling prey to lethal violence is low for men and women alike, men are still by far outweighing women on the offending side.

Also, honor killings (like hate killings) recently figure prominently in debates on violence against women and have been tabled internationally as the most severe manifestation of harmful practices which result in gender-based violence. While it is of course not disputed that honor killing establishes a homicide offence, this type of killing is also closely related to the issue of cultural defenses and the question of whether such acts deserve mitigated punishment (or even exemptions from punishment) in multicultural societies. Moreover, a high signal value can be attributed to honor violence. Raising the issue of honor killings triggers a signal that something (beyond the individual case) might have gone completely wrong and must be straightened out. Honor killings are easily loaded with the message that immigration policies went wrong, that multicultural and integration policies have failed, that human rights policies are not effective, and, most important, that honor killing expresses private punishment for breaking traditional cultural norms.

Another path of research on killing was opened in the last decades with emphasizing the use of deadly force by police or in detention places and assisted suicide and "compassionate"/mercy killing and establish fields of research fraught with a high potential of political mobilization.

No doubt, the study of *Violence in the Balkans* will serve as a solid basis for deepening further analysis of lethal violence and advancing significantly European homicide research due to the historical, political, and cultural particulars of the region.

Hans-Jörg Albrecht
Freiburg, Germany
March 27, 2021

Acknowledgments

Neither the *Balkan Homicide Study* (BHS) nor this book would have seen the light of day if it were not for the wholehearted commitment of Prof. Dr. Dr. h.c. mult. Hans-Jörg Albrecht to the Balkan region and my own scientific development. As the former director of the Max Planck Institute for Foreign and International Criminal Law in Freiburg (MPICC), he is not only cofounder of the BHS, but has also been my mentor and a benevolent patron to my academic career, and thus a precious source of inexhaustible inspiration. I am forever grateful for his sharp-witted guidance and generous support, but most of all for raising me to know that there are no ultimate disciplinary truths and that it is the very essence of a researcher's true nature to constantly challenge disciplinary paradigms.

Now, being anchored at a law faculty and imbedded in a rather conservative regional and academic setting, such challenging of disciplinary paradigms has never been easy, nor did it always go smoothly. For enduring my transdisciplinary undertakings and stubborn nature, while granting me the necessary space and support to follow my scientific aspirations, I am much obliged to Prof. Dr. Davor Derenčinović, the head of my faculty department and judge of the European Court of Human Rights.

In a project of this scale, thanks are due to too many people to list individually. Nevertheless, there is a core group of fellow researchers and friends from the Balkan Criminology Network, without whose commitment the BHS never would have been implemented successfully: Andra-Roxana Trandafir from Romania, Gorazd Meško and Rok Hacin from Slovenia, Gordana Lažetić from North Macedonia, Eszter Sárik and Orsolya Bolyky from Hungary, and Xhevdet Halili from Kosovo.

I wish to express my thanks to our generous funders: the MPICC, the University of Zagreb, my law faculty, the Croatian Science Foundation, and the Global Initiative against Transnational Organized Crime and its Resilience Fund.[1]

I would also like to sincerely thank all the members of my two research teams, the Balkan Criminology and Violence Research Lab, in particular Reana Bezić, Petra Šprem, and Dalia Pribisalić, who significantly contributed to the overall success of the BHS. Likewise, I would like to acknowledge the indispensable expert opinion and critical reflections of my peers, Marieke C.A. Liem and Goran Livazović, who kindly took the time for reviewing my manuscript.

Finally, without my husband Vanja's great sacrifice to act as our family's temporary stay-at-home dad, I never would have managed to conduct the BHS in-between two consecutive pregnancies, let alone to write this book. I thank him for his love and patience and for enabling me to do it all – to be a mum, a wife, and a researcher – and to do all of it passionately, without compromises.

[1] The MPICC provided the core funds for conducting the BHS, whereas the main workload of the study was carried out by the Balkan Criminology research group, first funded by the Max Planck Society from 2013 to 2019 and then by the Resilience Fund from 2019 onwards (www.balkan-criminology.eu). The open access publication is funded by the University of Zagreb, while the BHS data analysis has largely been conducted by the Violence Research Lab, established through the CroViMo project and co-funded by the Zagreb Faculty of Law and the Croatian Science Foundation (www.violence-lab.eu).

Contents

Chapter 1
Introduction to the Balkan Homicide Study

Abstract The *Balkan Homicide Study* (BHS) fills a considerable gap in current European homicide research. Its findings shed first light on the phenomenology of violence in this region of Europe. The BHS provides original empirical data from 2073 prosecution and court case files in six countries: Croatia, Hungary, Kosovo, North Macedonia, Romania, and Slovenia. By analyzing data on 2416 offenders and 2379 victims, the book at hand takes a close look at situational, criminogenic, victimogenic, and procedural characteristics of (lethal) violence in the Balkans. It thus investigates the highly heterogeneous types of different *(potentially) deadly situations*, thereby focusing on what might make them become deadly and what could be possible *protective traits* on the side of victims. Such an investigation of pathways into lethal violence becomes possible only if lethal violence (completed homicides) is studied together with non-lethal violence (attempted homicides). This approach however considerably broadens the subject and scope of homicide research, which commonly deals primarily with lethal violence. This chapter provides a brief overview of the pros and cons of such an approach and briefly sketches the study's background. It also discusses the relevance of the criminal justice's power to define violence, introduces the *Balkan-violence-paradox,* and presents the study's conceptual, as well as terminological framework.

Keywords Balkan homicide study · Violence research · Violence definition · Lethal violence · Homicide research

1.1 Background

Violence and the study of violence have been an inexhaustible source of my scientific and personal fascination over the past 20 years, and I am still deeply impressed by the writings of Wolfgang Sofsky (1996), Heinrich Popitz (1992), Trutz von Trotha (1997) and Trotha and Rösel (2011). Violence research has also been one of the main focuses of the Max Planck Partner Group for Balkan Criminology (BC) that I have been running from 2012 onwards. However, it was only in spring 2016,

© The Author(s) 2021
A.-M. Getoš Kalac, *Violence in the Balkans*, SpringerBriefs in Criminology,
https://doi.org/10.1007/978-3-030-74494-6_1

and after BC had already been heavily engaged in numerous large non-violence projects, like the ISRD3 (International Self-Report Delinquency Study), when Prof. Dr. Dr. h.c. mult. Hans-Jörg Albrecht and I started working on the research design for a study into (lethal) violence in the Balkans. Like many of our grand ideas *on* and *in* the Balkans, it all started out over a casual cup of coffee and a contemplating smoke.

Our preliminary analysis showed that in fact no recent or larger empirical violence study had been conducted in the majority of BC partner countries, especially none with a regionally comparative approach. In addition to this empirical vacuum, we also detected a considerable theoretical vacuum when it comes to explaining violence in the Balkans outside the framework of simply copy-pasting theories developed in other parts of the world.[1] Both the empirical and the theoretical vacuum called for our criminological engagement.

Based on a questionnaire Prof. Dr. Albrecht had already developed and tested for the study of lethal violence in Uruguay, we started working on the research design and questionnaire for the BHS (Sect. 4.2). In a next step, we selected several partner countries from the Balkan Criminology Network (BCNet) based on their geographical location in the region. In March 2016, together with the BHS partners and based on prior analysis of all the relevant national homicide statistics, we considerably broadened the initial Uruguay questionnaire and thus adjusted it to our study's research questions and the regional context. We thus decided on data sourcing and sampling strategies. Equipped with highly contagious enthusiasm and ample team spirit, as well as 5000€ on average for the field work, total data collection and analysis for each of the six participating countries,[2] the BHS was officially launched.

Our idea for the BHS has been to focus on two main lines of research. First, we were interested in capturing *violence as a normative and social construct*, in order to investigate the *power to define violence* and how it is used throughout the criminal justice system (Sessar, 1981; Hess, 2010; Dölling, 2015). This is still an understudied topic in violence research, especially in the Balkans, though its comprehension has a crucial impact on many methodological decisions, for instance, including or excluding attempts or non-homicidal violent offenses. Basically, the question is how and why at police level violent incidents are defined, for example, as (attempted) homicide or grave bodily injury (with lethal consequences), and how and why such initial definitions are redefined by the prosecution and the courts. This is not only a strictly normative question about the power to define violence by

---

[1] Compared to the United States and several commonwealth countries, the study of trends, patterns, and explanations of homicide has no long tradition in Europe (Liem & Pridemore, 2014, p. 527). Same applies to the Balkans with even less empirical research into lethal violence.

[2] Due to a limited project budget, we were not able to include all BCNet countries, but had initially selected six of them: Albania, Bosnia and Herzegovina, Croatia, North Macedonia, Serbia, and Turkey. However, later on, it turned out that partners from Albania, Bosnia and Herzegovina, and Turkey were not able to conduct the fieldwork, so partners from Hungary, Kosovo, Romania, and Slovenia joined the BHS instead. Out of these seven participating countries, data from six of them has been available at the time of writing this book, whereas the field work in Serbia is still ongoing with no indication whether the data will be made available eventually.

different criminal justice actors but also a fundamental criminological question, for example, about understanding *homicide drop-outs*: why and how do (attempted) homicide cases get lost in criminal justice processing? It is thus an extremely intriguing question about the normative construction of violence vs. its criminological reality.[3]

This brings us to BHS's second line of research: the *empirical reality of violence*. There is an obvious paradox concerning lethal violence in the Balkans. On the one hand, there is solid evidence that, compared to other parts of Europe, the Balkans do not fit the profile of a high crime region and appear to be much safer in terms of street and urban crime (UNODC, 2008; Aebi et al., 2010, 2014). On the other hand, there is also solid evidence about a higher propensity toward lethal violence in the Balkans (UNODC, 2011, 2013). Available data indicates higher homicide rates than in other European regions, even though more recently a declining trend is noticeable (UNODC, 2019b). But what do these homicide rates actually reveal, beyond the obvious mere incidence of homicides? We were intrigued by this *Balkan-violence-paradox*. Finding out what (lethal) violence in the Balkans actually looks like, in terms of its criminological reality, might help understand, perhaps even explain the paradox. It might thus provide the empirical starting point for future theoretical reflections.[4]

1.2   Conceptual Framework

The question about what violence is and how it should be understood is much more than just a simple matter of terminology or methodology. It is, or at least should be, a conscious, transparent, and well-founded conceptual decision, as it pretty much determines how one ought to approach violence as a research subject. This in turn has a major impact on methodology and consequently on the research findings as such. One of the many challenges in violence research is the chronic lack of a commonly accepted definition of violence (Heitmeyer & Hagan, 2003; Imbusch, 2002). Violence, just as the scientific as well as the general perception, of what violence actually is, has clearly changed over time (Aebi & Linde, 2016). Although the undisputable core of violence is the intentional infliction of physical harm upon another person (Popitz, 1992; Nadelmann, 1997), the continuous adding of further dimensions, such as psychological, verbal, economic, structural, symbolic, cyber,

---

[3] Worth mentioning in this context is the *dark figure of homicide*, but since it relates to a different type of discussion, the issue will be picked up again and in more detail at a later point (Sect. 4.1).

[4] *Karstedt*'s research, for instance, shows that bad governance in and of criminal justice, particularly when it comes to the rule of law, is related to higher homicide rates and thus makes citizens less safe from violence (Karstedt, 2018, p. 6). It investigates the potential of (political) institutions to account for comparative and cross-sectional differences in violence (Karstedt, 2015). Based on findings from our BHS case file analysis, this theoretical explanation could be further investigated in the region at hand.

and object-related, has blurred the picture and vastly broadened the subject scope of violence research. There is a clear trend toward indefinitely stretching the term violence, up to the point where currently almost everything is labeled as violence, and where eventually almost nothing presents itself as violence anymore (Meyer, 2002). It is at least questionable whether such a broadening of violence research's subject scope has actually contributed to a better understanding of violence.[5] Yet, when it comes to homicide research, it is quite clear (at least to me) that the focus should be on the *infliction of physical harm upon another person*. That is also pretty much the only thing that appears to be quite clear.

Violence as a Social Construct   Being in the business of criminological violence research almost inevitably requires one's daily confrontation with social and normative constructs of violence. Be it crime statistics or court file analysis, health statistics, or forensic reports, all of them are deeply rooted in their own perception of reality. So, for example, in (German) criminal law, lethal poisoning, even if causing no suffering to the victim, is commonly perceived as an aggravating circumstance to simply killing another person. It is an *insidious murder* (Ger. Mord), even if it is a woman poisoning her physically far superior husband against whom she would never stand a chance in a bare-knuckled life and death fight. Choking the life out of someone that could last for agonizing 5 minutes, however, might well be perceived as a *normal killing*, a manslaughter (Ger. Totschlag). But if the killer was provoked by the victim into a state of extreme rage, then even the most brutal massacre might be perceived as a *less severe case of manslaughter* (Ger. Minder schwerer Fall des Totschlags). And as if such teleological normative constructions of violence were not enough, all *cruelty killings* are considered, just as painless poisonings, simple cases of insidious murder (Ger. Mord), whereas *justified killings* or those lacking *criminal responsibility* or *culpability* are normatively not even perceived as violence (Getoš Kalac & Šprem, 2020; Cooney, 2009). Similar normative classifications of violence exist throughout Europe, as well as its southeastern part and the Balkans. Ultimately, none of these normative perceptions sufficiently consider the realities of violence and the victims' suffering, but they rather focus on everything else around it (e.g., supposed motive or potential justification).

If we were to rank the above examples by their criminological realities, the ranking would be exactly the other way around. Now, using such normative constructs and their classifications as the foundation for criminological research is surely very practical, even unavoidable if one sources data from criminal justice agencies that operate on the grounds of such normative constructs. It is however not at all meaningful, at least not if one aims to study the empirical realities of violence, rather than their normative (re)interpretation. Criminology has so far failed to provide its own authentic perception of violence and is still largely preoccupied with fitting its

---

[5] For a vivid example on the conceptual and terminological chaos caused by broadening the understanding of violence, see relevant definitions of *cyber* violence (Getoš Kalac, 2021).

research subject into purely normative constructs of violence.[6] The BHS is no exception in this regard, but based on its findings, first ideas on developing an *authentic criminological violence classification system*, as well as a *universal measure of violence*, are discussed (Chap. 6).

Violence as an Empirical Reality   Violence, understood as the infliction of physical harm upon another person, is a tangible and empirically capturable event. It exists in reality regardless of whether it has been reported or someone has been found guilty for having caused it. It also exists in reality regardless of its normative justifiability and excusability, or intent, negligence, and criminal responsibility. A wide range of highly valuable (criminological) conceptual and theoretical perspectives have been developed in an attempt to tackle the challenge of coherently framing violence.[7] However, criminology has in general and independently from criminal law thus far not been able to fully conceptualize violence as an empirical reality, although examples from other disciplines show this is both possible and feasible.[8] In criminology, we have even managed to successfully avoid such basic questions as who or what and why should be considered a victim of violence, by simply

---

[6] So, for example, the International Classification of Crime for Statistical Purposes (ICCS) defines homicide as "*unlawful* death inflicted upon a person with the *intent* to cause death or serious injury." Besides the objective element (killing of one person by another person), this definition also contains a subjective element deeply rooted in criminal law constructs (the presumed *intent* of the perpetrator) and thus a purely normative element (the *unlawfulness* of the perpetrator's action) (UNODC, 2019a, p. 7). Despite the sound justification of such a definitional approach, as well as its methodological and practical necessity, criminologically speaking, such conceptualization is predefined by normative constructs which have no empirical basis or justification. In fact, the very essence of the legal concept of intent is based on the "scientifically disproven metaphysical/philosophical notion of free will," whereas the criterion of unlawfulness simply replicates "the baseless theological beliefs and the arbitrary moral values that guide and dominate criminal law" (cit. Fattah, 2008, p. 146–147).

[7] *Karstedt* and *Eisner* in a special issue of the *International Journal of Conflict and Violence* investigate the possibilities of a general theory of violence (Karstedt & Eisner, 2009). Leading authorities in the field present a broad range of theoretical approaches toward a general theory of violence, including interaction theory (Collins, 2009), evolutionary theory (Eisner, 2009), theories of deviance and aggression (Felson, 2009), or general theories of crime and Situational Action Theory (Tittle, 2009; Wikström & Treiber, 2009), whereas others reject the possibility of ahistorical general theories of violence (Shaw, 2009) (Karstedt & Eisner, 2009, p. 5–6).

[8] *Gómez* et al. for the purpose of their study of the phylogenetic roots of human lethal violence, for instance, define lethal violence as deaths due to conspecifics, regardless of unlawfulness or intent or comparable normative constructs. Lethal violence includes all of the following: infanticide, cannibalism, inter-group aggression, and any other type of intraspecific killings in non-human mammals; war, homicide, infanticide, execution, and any other kind of intentional conspecific killing in humans (Gómez et al., 2016, p. 233). One can assume that by "intentional," the authors of the study do not imply the normative meaning of the word but rather refer to "deliberate," since the study makes no reference to law or any normative concepts.

adopting the relevant normative constructs. These constructs are however all but scientific or empirically grounded and sometimes even highly inconsistent.[9]

Apparently different research areas in criminology, including homicide research, have managed to operationally define the subject of their interest, without necessarily embedding it into an overarching definitional or conceptual framework.[10] Such operational definitions in homicide research commonly discuss various aspects of diverse normative concepts (e.g., premeditation, intent, negligence, unlawful abortion, assisted suicide, euthanasia, infanticide, assault leading to death, reckless driving, justified killings, attempt, or responsibility) and then operationally simply decide on including some and excluding others (Smit et al., 2012). With the BHS, we conceptually did not solve this issue, neither did we much discuss it, except for the issue of attempt. Since this is a far-reaching conceptual decision we made, it shall be briefly addressed.

Lethal Violence or Homicide Basically, the question is whether *homicide* is a unique phenomenon, something essentially different than *lethal violence* – the deadly outcome of *violence*. Depending on one's answer, research should either include or exclude the study of non-lethal violence (attempted homicides). With the BHS, we approached this question from two angles. First, in order to actually be able to deal with the "(lethal) violence-homicide dilemma" as such, one must include attempts (nonlethal violence) and then based on the findings determine if lethal violence is merely a subtype of violence, or whether it is a unique type of violence – homicide – which should be studied independently from attempts. Second, from a victimological perspective, it would be almost irresponsible not to search for potential protective traits on the side of victims and deescalating situational factors that might explain why some violence turns out deadly whereas other does not. While it is indeed plausible to exclude attempts from homicide statistics,

---

[9]A great example demonstrating the inconsistency of *normative victim constructs* and consequently their right to protection from violence is the prohibition of slaughtering pregnant mammals in the last third of their pregnancy in Germany. The official reasoning for the 2017 ban literary reads as follows: the *unborn animal* shall be protected from suffering and pain (Deutscher Bundestag, 2017). Now, if unborn mammals are normatively constructed as potential victims of violence, and as such protected from suffering and pain, then a consistent application of such a construct would imply its application to unborn human mammals as well. This is however not the case in Germany, where abortion is generally prohibited, but not in order to protect the unborn human from suffering and pain, but to protect the becoming life (Ger. Rechtsgut: das werdende Leben). Since the *unborn human* is normatively not constructed as a person (prior to the start of the birth process), it normatively cannot be considered a victim that would be entitled to protection from suffering and pain.

[10]Criminology's chronic lack of a perspective-defined grasp of its study subject, although problematic in the context discussed here, is not necessarily a disadvantage. Surely, criminology's lack of being perspective-defined might render it deficient in terms of disciplinary autonomy, but at the same time, its very nature of being problem-defined predestines it for transdisciplinarity, thereby providing it with a unique yet underutilized competitive advantage (Getoš Kalac, 2020).

particularly internationally comparable ones (UNODC, 2019a; Smit et al., 2012), homicide research that is based on case analysis should include attempts, just as it should include a wide range of various types of non-homicidal (lethal) violent events, in order to enable the interpretation of findings within their overall violent context.[11]

1.3   Terminology

There are several central terms relevant for the BHS, which need to be defined early on. The aim of clarifying the terminology used is not to provide for generally acceptable definitions but to provide for a common understanding of the key terms used throughout the book.

(Lethal) Violence and (Attempted) Homicide For the purpose of the book at hand with the term violence, the human infliction of physical harm upon another person is meant. The adjective lethal denotes that as a consequence of such violence another person has died. The person inflicting the violence is the offender, whereas the person suffering the violence is the victim, while the violent event is the incident. Since the term homicide is widely used, especially in English language and in the field of violence research (Smit et al., 2012, p. 8), (lethal) violence and (attempted) homicide are used interchangeably, without implying any essential uniqueness of homicide as a phenomenon.

Balkan or Southeast Europe The terms Balkan, Western Balkans, and Southeastern Europe and their common inconsistent usage cause much confusion. Whereas the term Western Balkans is neither academically nor historically justifiable and can be attributed to everyday political affairs, from a historical-structural perspective, one can differentiate between a *broader* concept of Southeast Europe and the *narrower* concept of the Balkans (Sundhaussen, 2014). Southeast Europe ranges from the western part of the former Kingdom of Hungary, the present Slovakia, over Hungary and the Republic of Moldova to approximately Odessa on the Black Sea, and everything that lies below this line is Southeast Europe (Sundhaussen, 2014). The Balkan, according to *Sundhaussen*, includes Bosnia and Herzegovina, Serbia (not including Vojvodina), Kosovo, Montenegro, North Macedonia, Bulgaria, the European part of Turkey (Eastern Thrace), Greece, and Albania, as well as the corridor between the Lower Danube and the Black Sea

---

[11] Conceptually the BHS would also have included assaults leading to death, as well as lethal consequences of numerous other criminal events (e.g. rape, robbery, or reckless driving), but this was simply not within the budget of the study. The Violence Research Lab takes such a broader and more holistic approach in an attempt to capture the empirical realities of (lethal) violence in Croatia (www.violence-lab.eu)

(Dobruja, split between Romania and Bulgaria) (2014, p. 8). Since the BHS in terms of sample countries covers four Southeast European and three Balkan states, one could argue for renaming BHS to SEEHS (Southeast European Homicide Study). However, since the violent Balkan images and stereotypes also frequently apply to the broader concept of Southeast Europe, as will be demonstrated later on (Sect. 3.1), the usage of the term Balkans remains justified. Similarly, the (criminological) research setting in the Balkans is quite comparable to that in Southeast Europe, whereas it is in many regards rather different to that found in most other European regions (Sect. 3.2). With this in mind, this book uses the terms Balkan and Southeastern Europe.

References

Aebi, M., & Linde, A. (2016). Long-term trends in crime: Continuity and change. In P. Knepper & A. Johansen (Eds.), *The Oxford handbook of the history of crime and criminal justice* (pp. 57–87). New York: Oxford University Press.

Aebi, M., et al. (2010). *European sourcebook of crime and criminal justice statistics* (4th ed.). The Hague: WODC.

Aebi, M., et al. (2014). *European sourcebook of crime and criminal justice statistics* (5th ed.). Helsinki: HEUNI.

Collins, R. (2009). Micro and macro theories of violence. *International Journal of Conflict and Violence, 3*(1), 9–22.

Cooney, M. (2009). *Is killing wrong? A study in pure sociology*. Charlottesville, London: University of Virginia Press.

Deutscher Bundestag. (2017). Bundestag verbietet Schlachtung trächtiger Rinder. https://www.bundestag.de/dokumente/textarchiv/2017/kw20-de-tierschutzrechtliche-vorschriften-505060. Accessed 19 Feb 2020.

Dölling, D. (2015). Zur Anwendung der Mordmerkmale in der Strafrechtspraxis. *Forensische Psychiatrie, Psychologie, Kriminologie, 9*(4), 228–235.

Eisner, M. (2009). The uses of violence: An examination of some cross-cutting issues. *International Journal of Conflict and Violence, 3*(1), 40–59.

Fattah, E. A. (2008). The future of criminology as a social science and academic discipline: Reflections on criminology's unholy alliance with criminal policy & on current misguided attempts to divorce victimology from criminology. *International Annals of Criminology, 46*(1/2), 137–170.

Felson, R. B. (2009). Violence, crime, and violent crime. *International Journal of Conflict and Violence, 3*(1), 23–39.

Getoš Kalac, A. M. (2020). Guilt, dangerousness and liability in the era of pre-crime – The role of criminology? To adapt, or to die, that is the question! *Monatsschrift für Kriminologie und Strafrechtsreform, 103*(3), 198–207.

Getoš Kalac, A. M. (2021). (Cyber) Bullying by faceless bureaucracy in research funding: A case study from the Balkans. In R. Haferkamp, M. Kilchling, J. Kinzig, D. Oberwittler, & G. Wößner (Eds.), *Unterwegs in Kriminologie und Strafrecht – Exploring the World of Crime and Criminology. Festschrift für Hans-Jörg Albrecht zum 70. Geburtstag* (pp. 511–540). Berlin: Duncker & Humblot. Extended preprint retrievable from https://www.bib.irb.hr/1054936. Accessed 20 Jan 2021.

Getoš Kalac, A. M., & Šprem, P. (2020). Kaznenopravno i kriminološko poimanje "delinkventnog" nasilja u Hrvatskoj. *Croatian Academy of Legal Sciences Yearbook, 11*(1), 119–132.

Gómez, J., Verdú, M., González-Megías, A., et al. (2016). The phylogenetic roots of human lethal violence. *Nature, 538*, 233–237.

Heitmeyer, W., & Hagan, J. (Eds.). (2003). *International handbook of violence research.* Dordrecht/Boston/London: Kluwer Academic Publishers.

Hess, A. (2010). *Erscheinungsformen und Strafverfolgung von Tötungsdelikten in Mecklenburg-Vorpommern.* Mönchengladbach: Forum-Verlag Godesberg.

Imbusch, P. (2002). Der Gewaltbegriff. In W. Heitmeyer & J. Hagan (Eds.), *Internationales Handbuch der Gewaltforschung* (pp. 26–57). Wiesbaden: Westdeutscher Verlag.

Karstedt, S. (2015). Does democracy matter? Comparative perspectives on violence and democratic institutions. *European Journal of Criminology, 12*(4), 457–481.

Karstedt, S. (2018). Is 'Big Picture Criminology' policy relevant? Comparative criminology, evidence-based policies and the scale of our discipline. *Criminology in Europe, 17*(3), 4–11.

Karstedt, S., & Eisner, M. (2009). Introduction: Is a general theory of violence possible? *International Journal of Conflict and Violence, 3*(1), 4–8.

Liem, M., & Pridemore, W. A. (2014). Homicide in Europe. *European Journal of Criminology, 11*(5), 527–529.

Meyer, T. (2002). Politische Kultur und Gewalt. In W. Heitmeyer & J. Hagan (Eds.), *Internationales Handbuch der Gewaltforschung* (pp. 1195–1214). Wiesbaden: Westdeutscher Verlag.

Nadelmann, B. (1997). Gewaltsoziologie am Scheideweg. Die Auseinandersetzungen in der gegenwärtigen und Wege der künftigen Gewaltforschung. In T. v. Trotha (Ed.), *Soziologie der Gewalt* (pp. 59–85). Opladen: Westdeutscher Verlag.

Popitz, H. (1992). *Phänomene der Macht.* Tübingen: J.C.B. Mohr.

Sessar, K. (1981). *Rechtliche und soziale Prozesse einer Definition der Tötungskriminalität.* Freiburg/Breisgau: Max-Planck-Institut für Ausländisches und Internationales Strafrecht.

Shaw, M. (2009). Conceptual and theoretical frameworks for organised violence. *International Journal of Conflict and Violence, 3*(1), 97–106.

Smit, P. R., de Jong, R. R., & Bijleveld, C. C. J. H. (2012). Homicide data in Europe: Definitions, sources, and statistics. In M. Liem & W. Pridemore (Eds.), *Handbook of European homicide research* (pp. 5–23). New York: Springer.

Sofsky, W. (1996). *Traktat über die Gewalt.* Frankfurt/Main: Fischer Verlag.

Sundhaussen, H. (2014). The Balkan Peninsula: A historical region *Sui Generis.* In A.-M. Getoš Kalac, H.-J. Albrecht, & M. Kilchling (Eds.), *Mapping the criminological landscape of the Balkans: A survey on criminology and crime with an expedition into the criminal landscape of the Balkans* (pp. 3–22). Berlin: Duncker & Humblot.

Tittle, C. (2009). Is a general theory of socially disapproved violence possible (or necessary)? *International Journal of Conflict and Violence, 3*(1), 60–74.

Trotha, T. V. (Ed.). (1997). *Soziologie der Gewalt.* Opladen: Westdeutscher Verlag.

Trotha, T. V., & Rösel J. (2011). On Cruelty. Köln: R. Köppe.

UNODC. (2008). *Crime and its impact on the Balkans and affected countries.* Vienna: UNODC.

UNODC. (2011). *Global study on homicide 2011.* Vienna: UNODC.

UNODC. (2013). *Global study on homicide 2013.* Vienna: UNODC.

UNODC. (2019a). *Global study on homicide 2019, booklet 1: Executive summary.* Vienna: UNODC.

UNODC. (2019b). *Global study on homicide 2019, booklet 2: Homicide: Extent, patterns, trends and criminal justice response.* Vienna: UNODC.

Wikström, H. P., & Treiber, K. (2009). Violence as situational action. *International Journal of Conflict and Violence, 3*(1), 75–96.

Chapter 2
Balkanisation in European Homicide Research

Abstract The past decade has seen a substantial growth of scholarly work on European homicide, combined with initiatives to systematically gather homicide data on a pan-European level. In this contribution, I will reflect on these initiatives, in particular on the construction of the European Homicide Monitor (EHM) and how it relates to other initiatives, such as the Balkan Homicide Study (BHS) described in the book at hand. To put initiatives such as the EHM and the BHS into empirical perspective, this contribution also provides an outline of prior and current research on homicide in Europe. Finally, I will reflect on some of the unique challenges that surround the empirical assessment of homicide in the Balkans.

Keywords Homicide · European Homicide Monitor · Methodology · Databases · Western Europe · Measurement · Overview

Marieke Liem is Professor of Violence and Interventions at Leiden University, where she and her team take part in the European Homicide Monitor, and are in charge of updating and maintaining the Dutch Homicide Monitor. A graduate of the University of Cambridge, she completed her PhD in Forensic Psychology from Utrecht University (cum laude). Before joining Leiden University, she was a Marie Curie fellow at Harvard University's Kennedy School of Government. Her research interests involve interpersonal violence, with specific research projects on domestic homicide (including intimate partner homicide), homicide by the mentally ill, homicide followed by suicide, the effects of confinement on violent offenders, and international comparative research on lethal violence.

Parts of this chapter have appeared in modified form in Liem, M. (2013) "A Brief History of the Future of European Homicide" in: *Criminology – Criminal Policy – Criminal Law. Evidence-Based Crime Control.* Schwarzenegger, C. & Kuhn, A. (eds.) Zurich: Stämpfli Publishers, and in Liem, M. (2017) "Homicide in Europe" in: International Handbook on Homicide. Brookman, F. & Maguire, M. & Maguire, E. (eds.) Chichester: Wiley & Sons.

© The Author(s) 2021   11
A.-M. Getoš Kalac, *Violence in the Balkans*, SpringerBriefs in Criminology,
https://doi.org/10.1007/978-3-030-74494-6_2

2.1 Homicide as a Yardstick

Homicide is generally considered the most serious of all crimes (Smit et al., 2012), and according to some, it constitutes the "tip of the iceberg" of underlying crime. In this view, homicide is the end result of lesser forms of crimes, such as robberies, rapes, and thefts (Ouimet & Montmagny-Grenier, 2014). The assumption is that different forms of crime are likely to share common causes, yet that police are much more likely to record homicides than other types of (non-lethal) crime (Lauritsen et al., 2016). From this line of reasoning, the homicide rate (reflecting the number of homicides per 100,000 population) is frequently used as an indicator of the level of violence in cross-national and historical studies (Nivette, 2011; Oberwittler, 2019; UNODC, 2019).

But there is another, more practical reason why homicide is frequently used as an indicator of the level of violence: It is seen as the most reliably measured of all crimes (Oberwittler, 2019; Pridemore, 2005). Homicides, unlike other (violent) crimes, leave a body behind, making this type of crime more visible and detectable by the authorities (Oberwittler, 2019; Ouimet & Montmagny-Grenier, 2014), regardless of reporting trends (Neapolitan, 1997). Other categories of crime data are thought to suffer from considerable validity problems (Neapolitan, 1997). More specifically, crimes of violence are not defined in the same way in different countries, and police also do not use the same thresholds of aggravation in the classification of violent offences in different countries. Additionally, police practices for recording crime are thought to be much more likely to affect nonlethal violent crimes than homicides (O'Brien, 1996). Against this backdrop, homicide data are believed to have a greater external validity than other types of crime (Andersson & Kazemian, 2018). Its lethal outcome and its universal condemnation make homicide particularly amenable to temporal (longitudinal) and cross-sectional (geographic) comparisons (UNODC, 2019).

Given its salience, it is perhaps surprising that for a long time, European comparative homicide research has remained a relatively marginal field. Compared to the United States and several commonwealth countries, Europe does not have a long tradition of studying homicide trends, patterns, and explanations (Liem, 2017). This may be due to the large differences that exist between European countries in legal definitions of and data sources on homicide. In addition, the overwhelming presence of the United States as reference point in studies on European homicide may have impeded comparative analyses within Europe (Granath et al., 2011; Liem et al. 2013). The past decade, however, saw a substantial body of new scholarly work on European homicide, combined with initiatives to systematically gather homicide data on a pan-European level (Liem, 2017). In this contribution, I will reflect on these initiatives; particularly, on the construction of the European Homicide Monitor (EHM) and how it relates to other initiatives, such as the Balkan Homicide Study (BHS) described in the book at hand. First, however, let me take the opportunity to provide a sketch of prior and current research on homicide in Europe, so that initiatives such as the EHM and BHS can be put into empirical perspective.

2.2   A Stocktaking of European Homicide Research

Research on homicide in Europe can roughly be divided into four clusters: sociological, historical, forensic, and descriptive studies (i.e., studying specific subtypes of homicide) (Granath et al., 2011). Next, I will provide a brief overview of each of these clusters.

Sociological Approaches to Homicide in Europe   One of the earliest accounts of sociological approaches to homicide in Europe can be traced back to the 1920s, when the Finnish scholar Verkko (1951) observed that the proportion of female homicide victims was higher when the overall homicide rate was low and vice versa. Homicides involving unrelated young males as offender and victim tended to be the most variable part. In other words, increases and decreases of homicide are typically explained by the prevalence of such male-to-male encounters. If male-to-male homicides increase, the proportions of other types of homicide (such as female homicide) tend to decrease. Similarly, if male-to-male homicides decrease, the relative proportion of other homicides increases (Kivivuori et al., 2012). Today, these laws are also known as "Verkko's laws" and can still be applied to explain regional and historical variations in homicide (e.g., Gartner & Jung, 2014; Silverman & Kennedy, 1987; Trägardh, Nilsson, Granath, & Sturup, 2016).

Contemporary sociological approaches to homicide in Europe tend to focus on how the causes of homicide are located in the socio-demographic structure of society as well as in the recurring temporal and spatial dimensions and dynamics of everyday life (for an overview, see Granath et al., 2011). Much of this European research is inspired by US colleagues, as scholars have examined to what extent US findings can be found in Europe, too (Kivivuori et al., 2014). Central themes in these sociological approaches include the role of substance abuse in lethal violence: alcohol (Bye, 2008, 2012) and drugs (Schönberger et al., 2018), as well as the link between economic deprivation and homicide (McCall & Nieuwbeerta, 2007). Yet another strand of sociological perspectives in homicide research focuses on the relationship between firearms and homicide. The notion of guns facilitating violence is the key assumption behind the strict regulation of gun ownership in most European countries (Krüsselmann et al. 2021a, b). In a recent systematic review, we found some European studies showing a clear decline once availability of firearms is restricted, while other studies indicated a limited effect on only a very specific subgroup, such as female victims, or national guards with weapons at home. Due to methodological inconsistencies and regional differences, conclusive evidence on the relationship between the two is still lacking (Krüsselmann et al., 2021).

Historical Approaches to Homicide in Europe Through historical analyses, scholars have been able to trace homicide figures in Europe back to the fifteenth century, when about 50 people per 100,000 were victimised in a homicide. Over the years, this figure decreased to about 1 per 100,000 – a downward trend that continued well into the twentieth century. Homicide rates in Western Europe have remained stable and low (below 2 per 100,000) until approximately the late 1960s. Starting in the early 1970s, homicide rates showed a slight increase throughout Europe, before decreasing again in the 1990s (Eisner & Nivette 2012). It has been argued that this increase can be attributed to an increase in homicides between young men in public places, who are often strangers to one another (Eisner, 2008). The overall European decrease in homicide rate in the early 1990s, in turn, could be explained by pan-Western cultural changes: around this time, pan-Western cultures were marked by an increased emphasis on self-control and more conservative cultural values. In their latest analysis of Western European homicide rates, Aebi and Linde (2014) hold that the increases and decreases of homicide can be seen as reflections from a change in lifestyle. They attribute the parallel trends in male and female victimisation since the 1960s to the integration of women into the labor market and the convergence of similar lifestyles by men and women. As a result, men and women are exposed to similar risks outside of their homes. From a lifestyle theory perspective, the decrease of homicide in the late 1990s could be attributed to the rapid development of computer technologies and the Internet, leading to an increase of time spent at home, especially for young people, and in turn, a lowered risk of homicide victimisation (Aebi & Linde, 2014; Aarten & Liem, 2021).

It is important to note that not all European countries followed this pattern: The homicide drop was particularly noticeable in Western European countries. Homicide levels in Eastern Europe remained relatively high and started to decline much later, while rates in southern European countries have converged to levels also found in Northern and Western Europe (Eisner, 2003). Recently, scholars from the Nordic countries have combined forces in generating a Historical Homicide Monitor that seeks to capture – much like the European Homicide Monitor (see later on) – individual-based and incident-based historical homicide data in a uniform way, allowing for international historical comparisons.

Forensic Approaches to Homicide A third line of research on homicide in Europe involves forensic approaches to homicide, in which the study of the role of mental illness in homicide is most pronounced. Several population-based studies in England (Flynn et al., 2011; Nielssen & Large, 2010; Swinson et al., 2011), Denmark (Brennan et al., 2000), Sweden, and Finland (Eronen et al., 1996; Tiihonen et al., 1997) revealed a higher prevalence of mental illness among homicide offenders compared to the general population (for an overview, see Aarten & Liem, 2021). Similar findings have been reported on the relationship between mental illness and *victims* of homicide in studies in Sweden (Crump et al., 2013) and Denmark (Hiroeh et al., 2001). Within the forensic approach to homicidal behaviour, numerous European studies have focused on specific subtypes of mental illness. Here, the focus lies on the association between psychotic disorders, such as schizophrenia, and homicidal behaviour (Fazel et al., 2010; Sturup & Lindqvist, 2014; Vinkers & Liem, 2011). Each of these studies have taken a national perspective, describing the nature and incidence of the relationship between severe mental illness and homicide in separate countries. With the exception of several meta-analyses (Fazel, Gulati, Linsell, Geddes, & Grann, 2009; Nielssen & Large, 2010) that include various European countries other than Western countries, studies based on pan-European data are virtually absent.

Descriptive Approaches to Subtypes of Homicide The fourth set of studies on homicide in Europe is also the most voluminous and the most rapidly growing (Kivivuori et al., 2014). These studies focus on specific subtypes of homicide, in which research on domestic homicide is well represented. This predominantly includes research on intimate partner homicide (for a detailed overview, see Corradi and Stöckl (2014)) and child homicide. Studies in the latter category mostly rely on forensic-psychiatric, rather than national, data (Vanamo, Kauppi, Karkola, Merikanto, & Räsänen, 2001; Liem & Koenraadt, 2008). Homicide followed by suicide constitutes another homicide subtype that has been studied in European countries separately (Flynn et al., 2009; Kivivuori & Lehti, 2003; Liem et al., 2009; Shiferaw et al., 2010) as well as several countries combined (Liem et al., 2011). Finally, due to their low prevalence in Europe, studies on other subtypes of homicide, such as sexual homicides, are rare (Greenall & Richardson, 2015; Häkkänen-Nyholm et al., 2009) or, such as in the case of serial homicides, virtually absent and limited to anecdotal accounts.

2.3   The European Homicide Monitor

The overview sketched above illustrates at least two main characteristics in European Homicide research, captured in what I would term the *Balkanisation* of European Homicide Research: first, the vast heterogeneity in types of studies and, closely related to that, the diversity in types of data that have been used in these studies. Due to the heterogeneity in sources, forensic mental health data cannot be one-on-one compared to data focusing on a specific type of homicide, which in turn cannot be one-on-one compared to historical data and so on. At the same time, existing international comparative studies on homicide conducted by large organisations, such as the UNODC or WHO, rely on aggregated national data. Such aggregated data, however, do not allow for detailed, individual-based, or case-based analyses. These aggregated data alone, in other words, do not tell us anything about potential international differences in motives, relationships between victim and perpetrator, and the context in which the homicide takes place.

To overcome these limitations, together with European colleagues from Finland and Sweden, we developed and launched the European Homicide Monitor (EHM) (Granath et al., 2011) about ten years ago. The EHM framework follows a uniform structure (same variables and values) that allows individual participating countries to code homicide data in a comparable format. Together, the EHM captures detailed incident, and victim and perpetrator characteristics. Since its inception, aside from the Netherlands, Finland, and Sweden, the EHM is now also applied in Estonia, Denmark, Paris, Scotland, Switzerland, and the Dutch Caribbean. Participating countries have previously transformed their primary data into the uniform EHM structure to allow for comparative analyses, showcasing the potential of this framework to be used in studying international trends (Suonpää et al., forthcoming), urban homicide (Krüsselmann et al., 2021), homicide clearance (Liem et al., 2018), the role of firearms in homicide (Krüsselmann et al., 2021), and specific types of homicide (Liem et al., 2017; Liem et al., 2013). In recent years, a slightly modified form of the European Homicide Monitor has also been applied to study homicide in the Nordic countries (Lehti et al., 2019).

Using the European Homicide Monitor as a standardised coding instrument is not, however, without shortcomings. The first, and perhaps the most important one, is that the types of data we rely on for homicide research are not initially collected for the purposes of research (Marshall & Block, 2004). Police files, for example, are drawn up for investigative purposes, typically in a diary type of way, where, during the investigation, "witnesses" may become "persons of interest," who may ultimately become suspects. Filtering out information relevant for research purposes from such diary-oriented police systems constitutes one of the challenges. Similarly, other primary homicide data sources such as prosecution files, court transcripts, and autopsy reports and newspaper articles are not written with a research aim in mind. Not only do these sources differ in respect to their focus on the homicide incident (such as news reports), the victim (autopsy files), or the offender (criminal justice files), but consequently they also apply a different idiom to refer to these events: "death caused by exsanguination" in a coroner's report may in other documentation be referred to as "died as a result of a gunshot wound," which in a newspaper be reported as "victim died in a shooting" and in a court transcript reflected as "sentenced for second-degree murder." Even though ideally we would apply and merge multiple data sources to verify the validity of the data at hand, this is oftentimes not possible. This leaves us with the challenge of finding a balance between coding cases from different sources according to a common denominator, without valuable details being lost.

The second key challenge concerns the coding of data. Coding, simply put, involves the transformation of narrative descriptions into an alphanumeric designation. The issue of coding becomes relevant when previously collected and previously coded homicide data are combined, such as in the European Homicide Monitor. Leaving aside the definitional issues that surround homicide – aspects that are almost universally coded are gender and age of the victim. Even though the EHM coding manual (see, for a detailed description: www.europeanhomicide.com) constitutes a comprehensive tool to code in a consistent and uniform manner, the recoding of other variables, which on the surface may appear to be straightforward and culturally homogeneous, becomes challenging when using data that were collected from a particular (non-research oriented) data source. A key example includes the variable *motive*: A newspaper report may reflect very different on the motive underlying the event when citing bereaved family members, compared to a police report, or to a forensic mental health evaluation of the suspect. Further, in its current form, the European Homicide Monitor coding scheme tends towards a lowest common denominator, the best example concerning "other" types of homicide: Next to pre-defined categories such as "homicides committed during robberies," "homicides in the criminal milieu," or "intimate partner homicides," the EHM contains a category for "other" homicides. In one of our early studies using the EHM, this has resulted in 46 per cent of all Finnish homicides, 23 per cent of all Dutch homicides, and 20 per cent of all Swedish homicides in our combined dataset to be coded as "other" (Granath et al., 2011; Liem et al., 2011) – a result, one could argue, of recoding existing data into homogeneous categories tended towards a lowest common denominator. One example includes homicides occurring at night in Finland, for example, that are often preceded and precipitated by heavy drinking by both victim and offender, in a kitchen setting. Quantitative data alone do not allow for the reflection of such specific settings and contexts. Other examples of country-specific and culture-specific settings of homicide that should be maintained because of their cultural uniqueness include mafia-related homicides in Italy, homicides in groups of temporary workers in Western Europe, honour-related killings among immigrant groups, and so on. One of the lessons learned from working on the European Homicide Monitor is to allow for these unique settings: leaving room for a short descriptive (string) variable with room for a short narrative on the specific case. In this way, we will be better able to capture the cultural and contextual uniqueness of homicide cases in each country.

Another challenge we face when using and analysing data from the European Homicide Monitor concerns missing data. The EHM is not unique in this – missingness is a researcher's curse encountered in many other large homicide datasets, including the FBI's Supplementary Homicide Reports (SHR) (Fox, 2004), the National Violent Death Reporting System (NVDRS) (Logan et al., 2009), and the Chicago Homicide Dataset (Block & Block, 1998), to name a few. The most prominent type of missingness in data pertains to detailed offender and victim characteristics as well as to victim-offender relationship (Fox, 2004). Accurately documenting patterns and trends in homicide rates distinguished by the relationship between perpetrators and victims is an important issue for the epidemiology of crime in Europe. The extent of domestic and intimate partner homicides relative to acquaintance and stranger homicides tells us much about the nature of violent crime in Europe, how it differs across countries, and how it is changing over time. Yet, missing data compromise the ability to reach theoretically relevant conclusions about the context and meaning of homicide rates (Pampel & Williams, 2000). One reason for missingness in the European Homicide Monitor and other datasets alike concerns unsolved cases. An unknown offender implies an unknown motive, unknown circumstances, and an unknown victim-offender relationship (Liem et al., 2018). A persistent misconception in homicide research is that the "unknowns" in the victim/offender relationship variable are stranger homicides because this type of homicide is more difficult to clear by arrest than those in which victims knew their offenders. Decker (1993), however, showed that stranger homicides do not account for many homicides classified as unknown relationships; indeed, they may be distributed among uncleared cases in the same proportions as they are among cleared homicide cases.

Even though several statistical solutions have been applied previously in large-scale homicide databases – including imputation-based procedures, weighting procedures, and model-based procedures (Riedel & Regoeczi, 2004) – imputed data do not have the same standing as observed data. Statistical solutions for missing data are no substitute for data collection that results in no missing values (Riedel & Regoeczi, 2004). The solution, hence, lies in the minimisation of missingness by going back to the source. In further developing the European Homicide Monitor, this should be achieved by consulting additional data sources and by making efforts to follow up on homicides that are solved at a later stage and, therefore, are able to provide background information at a later stage. Another solution has been applied in the National Violent Death Reporting System (CDC, 2020) data coding process. Today, the NVDRS operates in all 50 US states. As states have joined in one by one, over the years, research staff provides training sessions and guidance to adequately code and enter data in the NVDRS software manual. Though costly, this elaborate process does not only decrease the occurrence of missing data from the bottom up but also strengthens the internal validity of the data. In further developing the European Homicide Monitor, we should learn from the wheel others invented before us when assembling large datasets, while at the same time reshaping this wheel according to the unique European – including Balkan – context.

Finally, in its present form, the European Homicide Monitor spans – in some countries – more than two decades, allowing for unique trend analyses. At the same time, we continue to encourage other countries to join this initiative and encourage other research fields to reap the benefits of this data coding and data collection endeavour. Examples include current projects on firearm homicide, in the context of illegal firearms trafficking (Project TARGET; and for an overview see, for example, Krüsselmann et al., 2021), and drug-related homicide, in the context of drug-related crime (Schönberger et al., 2018). To lower the threshold of applying the EHM structure in such affiliated projects, we now also offer a user-friendly, condensed nucleus set of 25 variables that capture the most important and readily retrievable victim, offender, and case characteristics (for an overview, see www.europeanhomicide.com).

2.4   Unique Challenges in a Balkanised Setting

The BHS team sought to overcome similar problems as we faced in developing and applying the European Homicide Monitor. This included, but was certainly not limited to, a lack of unified reporting system throughout the Balkans, a lack of a unified definition, and cultural-linguistic differences. However, there are some unique challenges involved in doing homicide research in the Balkans that deserve closer consideration. First, while criminology as a discipline has grown into a rich, versatile, and independent field of study in many Western and Northern European countries, this is not the case in the Balkans. This vacuum is reflected in the criminological research capacities, which are almost exclusively situated at universities. Second, criminological research in the area seems to focus on national rather than comparative issues. Further, as opposed to the Western and Northern European countries, most criminological studies are state-funded, with relatively few national or regional foundations that fund criminological research. Against this background, there is little experience in conducting homicide research specifically to such an extent that the BHS team struggled with a lack of experience and guidance on aspects such as sampling, recruiting, and training of field workers, as well as case analysis, quality control, and so on. In one of our many conversations on how to navigate these difficulties, Anna-Maria Getoš Kalac, the author of the book that lays before you, summarised the approach taken as "learning by doing" – yet learning the hard way.

These challenges, taken together, have made it very difficult to compare the findings from the BHS to studies conducted outside of the region. In moving forward, I can only encourage the BHS team to join the well-proven concept of the European Homicide Monitor (EHM). Despite its initial start-up challenges, the European Homicide Monitor has now expanded beyond the initial three pilot countries, and in regular feedback loops, we continue to improve it over time. These factors taken together, the EHM promises to be an even richer data source in the future to be used by researchers and policy makers. As I have discussed in this overview, despite the central need for sound knowledge on lethal violence, most EU countries, including the Balkan countries, lack well-developed data of the kind that is required for reliable assessments. Further developing the European Homicide Monitor can fill these lacunae. Such developments, I feel, go hand in hand with combining forces in sharing practices and lessons learned in successfully conducting comparative multi-country homicide studies. This does not only include sharing experiences in designing and conducting research based on a broad exchange of experiences but also involve opening the discussion on cultural aspects in homicide research. Expanding and combining our data collection efforts can provide unique opportunities to follow and make assessments of trends and factors that foster lethal violence, as well as preventive measures, sentencing policies and the treatment of perpetrators from a pan-European perspective. It is my hope that this would greatly improve the opportunities for EU-level initiatives to work in different ways to reduce the burden of lethal violence.

References

Aarten, P. G., & Liem, M. C. (2021). Unravelling the Homicide Drop: Disaggregating a 25-Year Homicide Trend in the Netherlands. European Journal on Criminal Policy and Research, 1–26.

Aebi, M., & Linde, A. (2014). The persistence of lifestyles: Rates and correlates of Homicide in Western Europe from 1960 to 2010. *European Journal of Criminology, 11*(5), 552–577.

Andersson, C., & Kazemian, L. (2018). Reliability and validity of cross-national homicide data: A comparison of UN and WHO data. *International Journal of Comparative and Applied Criminal Justice, 42*(4), 287–302.

Block, C. R., & Block, R. L. (1998). *Homicides in Chicago 1965–1995*. Ann Arbor: ICPSR.

Brennan, P. A., Mednick, S. A., & Hodgins, S. (2000). Major mental disorders and criminal violence in a Danish birth cohort. *Archives of General Psychiatry, 57*(5), 494–500.

Bye, E. K. (2008). Alcohol and homicide in Eastern Europe a time series analysis of six countries. *Homicide Studies, 12*(1), 7–27.

Bye, E. K. (2012). Alcohol and homicide in Europe. In M. Liem & W. A. Pridemore (Eds.), *Handbook of European homicide research* (pp. 231–245). New York: Springer.

CDC. (2020). *NVDRS state profiles*. https://www.cdc.gov/violenceprevention/datasources/nvdrs/ stateprofiles.html. Accessed 17 Dec 2020.

Corradi, C., & Stöckl, H. (2014). Intimate partner homicide in 10 European countries: Statistical data and policy development in a cross-national perspective. *European Journal of Criminology, 11*(5), 601–618.

Crump, C., Sundquist, K., Winkleby, M. A., & Sundquist, J. (2013). Mental disorders and vulnerability to homicidal death: Swedish Nationwide cohort study. *British Medical Journal, 346*, 1–8.

Decker, S. H. (1993). Exploring victim-offender relationships in homicide: The role of individual and event characteristics. *Justice Quarterly, 10*, 585–612.

Eisner, M. (2003). Long-term historical trends in violent crime. *Crime and Justice, 30*, 83–142.

Eisner, M. (2008). Modernity strikes Back? A historical perspective on the latest increase in interpersonal violence (1960–1990). *International Journal of Conflict and Violence, 2*(2), 288–316.

Eisner, M., & Nivette, A. (2012). How to reduce the global homicide rate to 2 per 100,000 by 2060. In R. Loeber & B. C. Walsh (Eds.), *The future of criminology* (pp. 219–228). New York: Oxford University Press.

Eronen, M., Hakola, P., & Tiihonen, J. (1996). Mental disorders and homicidal behavior in Finland. *Archives of General Psychiatry, 53*(6), 497–501.

Fazel, S., Buxrud, P., Ruchkin, V., & Grann, M. (2010). Homicide in discharged patients with schizophrenia and other psychoses: A national case-control study. *Schizophrenia Research, 123*(2–3), 263–269.

Fazel, S., Gulati, G., Linsell, L., Geddes, J. R., & Grann, M. (2009). Schizophrenia and violence: systematic review and meta-analysis. PLoS medicine, 6(8), e1000120.

Flynn, S., Swinson, N., While, D., Hunt, I. M., Roscoe, A., Rodway, C., Windfuhr, K., Kapur, N., Appleby, L., & Shaw, J. (2009). Homicide followed by suicide: A cross-sectional study. *Journal of Forensic Psychiatry and Psychology, 20*(2), 306–321.

Flynn, S., Abel, K. M., While, D., Mehta, H., & Shaw, J. (2011). Mental illness, gender and homicide: A population-based descriptive study. *Psychiatry Research, 185*(3), 368–375.

Fox, J. A. (2004). Missing data problems in the SHR. *Homicide Studies, 8*(3), 214–254.

Gartner, R., & Jung, M. (2014). Sex, gender, and homicide: Contemporary trends and patterns. In R. Gartner & B. McCarthy (Eds.), The Oxford handbook of gender, sex and crime (pp. 424–447). Oxford University Press.

Granath, S., Hagstedt, J., Kivivuori, J., Lehti, M., Ganpat, S., Liem, M., & Nieuwbeerta, P. (2011). *Homicide in Finland, the Netherlands and Sweden*. A first study on the European Homicide Monitor data. Swedish Council for Crime Prevention. Stockholm: Bra.

Greenall, P. V., & Richardson, C. (2015). Adult male-on-female stranger sexual homicide a descriptive (baseline) study from Great Britain. *Homicide Studies, 19*(3), 237–256. https://doi. org/10.1177/1088767914530555

Häkkänen-Nyholm, H., Repo-Tiihonen, E., Lindberg, N., Salenius, S., & Weizmann-Henelius, G. (2009). Finnish sexual homicides: Offence and offender characteristics. *Forensic Science International, 188*(1–3), 125–130.

Hiroeh, U., Appleby, L., Mortensen, P. B., & Dunn, G. (2001). Death by homicide, suicide, and other unnatural causes in people with mental illness: A population-based study. *The Lancet, 358*(9299), 2110–2112.

Kivivuori, J., & Lehti, M. (2003). Homicide followed by suicide in Finland: Trend and social locus. *Journal of Scandinavian Studies in Criminology and Crime Prevention, 4*(2), 223–236.

Kivivuori, J., Savolainen, J., & Danielsson, P. (2012). Theory and explanation in contemporary European homicide research. In M. Liem & W. Pridemore (Eds.), *Handbook of European homicide research* (pp. 95–109). New York: Springer.

Kivivuori, J., Suonpaa, K., & Lehti, M. (2014). Patterns and theories of European homicide research. *European Journal of Criminology, 11*(5), 530–551.

Krüsselmann, K., Aarten, P., Ahven, A., d'Arbois de Jubainville, H., Granath, S., Langlade, A., Lehti, M., Markwalder, N., Thomsen, A., Walser, S., & Liem, M. (2021a). *Firearm-related homicides in Europe*. Manuscript in preparation.

Krüsselmann, K., Aarten, P., Ahven, A., Granath, S., Langlade, A., Lehti, M., Markwalder, N., Thomsen, A., Walser, S., & Liem, M. (2021b). *A spatial examination of homicides types in Europe*. Manuscript in preparation.

Krüsselmann, K., Aarten, P., & Liem, M. (2021). Firearms and violence in Europe–A systematic review. PloS one, 16(4), e0248955.

Lauritsen, J. L., Rezey, M. L., & Heimer, K. (2016). When choice of data matters: Analyses of US crime trends, 1973–2012. *Journal of Quantitative Criminology, 32*(3), 335–355.

Lehti, M., Bergsdóttir, G. S., Granath, S., Jónasson, J. O., Kivivuori, J., Liem, M., Okholm, M. M., Rautelin, M., & Suonpää, K. (2019). *Nordic Homicide Report. Homicide in Denmark, Finland, Iceland, Norway and Sweden, 2007–2016*. Helsinki: KRIMO.

Liem, M. (2013). A brief history of the future of European homicide. In C. Schwarzenegger & A. Kuhn (Eds.), *Criminology – Criminal policy – Criminal law. Evidence-based crime control*. Zurich: Stämpfli Publishers.

Liem, M. (2017). Homicide in Europe. In F. Brookman, M. Maguire, & E. Maguire (Eds.), *International handbook on homicide*. Chichester: Wiley.

Liem, M., & Koenraadt, F. (2008). Familicide: A comparison with spousal and child homicide. *Criminal Behaviour and Mental Health, 18*, 306–318.

Liem, M., Postulart, M., & Nieuwbeerta, P. (2009). Homicide-suicide in the Netherlands an epidemiology. *Homicide Studies, 13*(2), 99–123.

Liem, M., Barber, C., Markwalder, N., Killias, M., & Nieuwbeerta, P. (2011). Homicide-suicide and other types of violent death in three countries. *Forensic Science International, 207*, 70–76.

Liem, M., Ganpat, S., Granath, S., Hagstedt, J., Kivivuori, J., Lehti, M., & Nieuwbeerta, P. (2013). Homicide in Finland, the Netherlands, and Sweden: First findings from the European homicide monitor. *Homicide Studies, 17*(1), 75–95.

Liem, M., Kivivuori, J., Lehti, M., Granath, S., & Schönberger, H. (2017). Les homicides conjugaux en Europe: résultats provenant du European homicide monitor [intimate partner homicide in Europe: Findings from the European homicide monitor]. *Les Cahiers de la Sécurité, 41*(3), 134–146.

Liem, M., Suonpää, K., Lehti, M., Kivivuori, J., Granath, S., Walser, S., & Killias, M. (2018). Homicide clearance in Western Europe. *European Journal of Criminology, 16*(1), 81–101.

Logan, J. E., Karch, D. L., & Crosby, A. E. (2009). Reducing "unknown" data in violent death surveillance: A study of death certificates, coroner/medical examiner and police reports from the National Violent Death Reporting System, 2003-2004. *Homicide Studies, 13*(4), 385–397.

Marshall, I. H., & Block, C. R. (2004). Maximizing the availability of cross-national data on homicide. *Homicide Studies, 8*(3), 267–310.

McCall, P. L., & Nieuwbeerta, P. (2007). Structural covariates of homicide rates: A European City cross-national comparative analysis. *Homicide Studies, 11*(3), 167.

Neapolitan, J. L. (1997). Homicides in developing nations: Results of research using a large and representative sample. *International Journal of Offender Therapy and Comparative Criminology, 41*(4), 358–374.

Nielssen, O., & Large, M. (2010). Rates of homicide during the first episode of psychosis and after treatment: A systematic review and meta-analysis. *Schizophrenia Bulletin, 36*(4), 702–712.

Nivette, A. E. (2011). Cross-national predictors of crime: A meta-analysis. *Homicide Studies, 15*(2), 103–131.

Oberwittler, D. (2019). Lethal violence: A global view on homicide. In *Oxford research encyclopedia of criminology and criminal justice*. Oxford University Press.

O'Brien, R. M. (1996). Police productivity and crime rates: 1973-1992. *Criminology, 34*(2), 183–207.

Ouimet, M., & Montmagny-Grenier, C. (2014). "Homicide and Violence—International and Cross-National Research": The construct validity of the results generated by the world homicide survey. *International Criminal Justice Review, 24*(3), 222–234.

Pampel, F. C., & Williams, K. R. (2000). Intimacy and homicide: Compensating for missing data in the SHR. *Criminology, 38*(2), 661–680.

Pridemore, W. A. (2005). A cautionary note on using county-level crime and homicide data. *Homicide Studies, 9*(3), 256–268.

Riedel, M., & Regoeczi, W. C. (2004). Missing data in homicide research. *Homicide Studies, 8*(3), 163–192.

Schönberger, H., Liem, M., Kivivuori, J., Lehti, M., Granath, S., & Suonpää, K. (2018). *Drug-related homicide in Europe: A pilot study*. Lisbon: EMCDDA Papers.

Shiferaw, K., Burkhardt, S., Lardi, C., Mangin, P., & La Harpe, R. (2010). A half century retrospective study of homicide-suicide in Geneva--Switzerland: 1956-2005. *Journal of Forensic and Legal Medicine, 17*(2), 62–66.

Silverman, R. A., & Kennedy, L. W. (1987). Relational distance and homicide: The role of the stranger. Journal of Criminal Law and Criminology, 78(2), 272–308.

Smit, P. R., de Jong, R. R., & Bijleveld, C. C. (2012). Homicide data in Europe: Definitions, sources, and statistics. In M. Liem & W. Pridemore (Eds.), *Handbook of European homicide research* (pp. 5–23). New York: Springer.

Sturup, J., & LindqvisT, P. (2014). Psychosis and homicide in Sweden—A time trend analysis 1987—2006. *International Journal of Forensic Mental Health, 13*(1), 1–7.

Suonpää, K., Kivivuori, J., Lehti, M., Aarten, P., Ahven, A., Granath, S., Markwalder, N., Skott, S., Thomsen, A., Walser, S., & Liem, M. (forthcoming). The homicide drop in seven European Countries: General or specific across countries and crime types?.

Swinson, N., Flynn, S. M., While, D., Roscoe, A., Kapur, N., Appleby, L., & Shaw, J. (2011). Trends in rates of mental illness in homicide perpetrators. *The British Journal of Psychiatry : the Journal of Mental Science, 198*(6), 485–489.

Tiihonen, J., Isohanni, M., Räsänen, P., Koiranen, M., & Moring, J. (1997). Specific major mental disorders and criminality: A 26-year prospective study of the 1996 Northern Finland Birth Cohort. *The American Journal of Psychiatry, 154*(6), 840–845.

Trägardh, K., Nilsson, T., Granath, S., & Sturup, J. (2016). A time trend study of Swedish male and female homicide offenders from 1990 to 2010. International Journal of Forensic Mental Health, 15(2), 125–135.

UNODC. (2019). *Global study on homicide*. Vienna: UNODC.

Vanamo, T., Kauppi, A., Karkola, K., Merikanto, J., & Räsänen, E. (2001). Intra-familial child homicide in Finland 1970–1994: incidence, causes of death and demographic characteristics. Forensic science international, 117(3), 199–204.

Verkko, V. (1951). *Homicides and suicides in Finland and their dependence on national character*. Copenhagen: C.F.C. Gads Forlag.

Vinkers, D., & Liem, M. (2011). Psychosis and homicide. *Psychiatric Services, 62*(10), 1234–1234.

Chapter 3
Criminological Violence Research in the Balkans: Context and Setting

Abstract The Balkans may very well be considered a criminological space *sui generis*. As a whole, the region shares more common traits internally than it does externally towards its European context. Therefore, it is necessary to explain the region's particularities, as relevant for understanding (lethal) violence and criminological research more generally speaking. The purpose of this chapter is to embed the BHS and its key findings in their Balkan-specific historical, religious, legal, and criminal justice context, while providing insights into the region's criminological research setting. After having read through this chapter, one should be able to understand not only the challenges but also the benefits of conducting criminological research in the Balkans. One should thus be able to mentally explore the region as a kind of criminologically uncharted territory in order to map its full potential for the further study of crime and harmful behavior – both, with regard to homicide research and countless other criminological topics. Doing empirical research *in* and *on* the Balkans is in practice extremely challenging and exhausting, as we shall see, but at the same time proves to be tremendously rewarding, especially if one considers research to be an adventure and oneself a discoverer.

Keywords Balkan history · Balkan stereotypes · Criminal state capture · Balkan research setting

3.1 Historical, Cultural, and Legal Context[1]

When looking at the Balkans from a criminological perspective, one needs to understand certain basics of its historical, cultural, and legal legacy, as well as its current criminal justice context. Moreover, with regard to homicide research, it is essential to recognize common Balkan images and stereotypes that frequently portray the

---

[1] This section is largely based on *Sundhaussen*'s analysis of "The Balkan Peninsula: A Historical Region *Sui Generis*." Since he is not only one of *the* ultimate authorities on the topic, but his analysis has also been tailor-fit to the needs of conducting criminological research into the region

© The Author(s) 2021

A.-M. Getoš Kalac, *Violence in the Balkans*, SpringerBriefs in Criminology,
https://doi.org/10.1007/978-3-030-74494-6_3

region as wild and violence prone, largely due to the rather recent post-Yugoslavian wars of 1991–1999. Obviously, the following discourse will need to be limited to selected key aspects deemed most relevant for providing context to the BHS. Therefore, we will have a brief look at violent images and stereotypes of the Balkans, followed by an overview of common traits that make the Balkans a historical space of its own kind, before discussing major religious, legal, cultural and criminal justice features that characterize the region as a distinctive criminological space.

3.1.1   Violent Balkan Images and Stereotypes

Much could be said about Balkan images, identities, and stereotypes,[2] but in an attempt to boil it all down to one vivid impression (Fig. 3.1), an example should provide for some remedy:

> **"Time for a slivovitz** I was sitting over dinner with three women about ten kilometers east of Belgrade: my Serbian girlfriend, her sister and her sister's daughter. The men of the family – two brothers, two cousins – were in the city, and all of them were armed because one of the brothers had almost been attacked by an enemy family. Luckily the police turned up in time. This had occurred in the afternoon, and it was now evening. My girlfriend's sister explained how it all started. A couple of years ago, drinking at his local, her husband's brother offered to buy a drink for a man who didn't like him. When the man scornfully declined, her brother in law pulled a gun and shot him in the leg, whereupon he went to prison for two years. Two weeks ago, he was released, and this afternoon, promptly ran into the man he had shot, surrounded by a group of friends. The house we were in stood all by itself, surrounded by snow. It snowed here day and night. The thought of what might happen next flashed through my mind. Instead of the men returning home, would their enemies come for the women? What would I do then? I had not spoken aloud, but the women read

Fig. 3.1 Time for a slivovitz (Möller-Kaya, 2016)

---

in question, further referencing proves redundant. Instead, the interested reader is invited to consult the analysis in question, as well as the references therein (Sundhaussen, 2014).

[2] On (violent) Balkan images, identities, and stereotypes in the context of political violence and radicalization, see, for example, Getoš (2012), pp. 84–103, and the numerous references therein.

my thoughts. "I think Helge needs a slivovitz," my girlfriend's sister said. Then she thought I might need a second one. I helped myself to a third, and by the seventh glass, I was on my feet declaring that they would be fine because I would protect them. I was itching for a fight with a couple of Serbs. That's when my girlfriend's sister said: I think Helge's had enough now. Nothing happened, of course. Nobody met anybody in town, and the men all came home in one piece. I'm only telling this story to explain what slivovitz does to you." (cit. Timmerberg, 2016)

The cited text is a feuilleton published together with the illustration rather recently in one of Lufthansa's magazines that is distributed globally on all its flights. It portraits an image, actually a violent stereotype, of the Balkans, as a region inhabited by "clan people," prone to wild, violent, and revengeful behavior, all together embedded in a culture of drinking slivovitz[3], while running around with guns, and shooting at each other for no good reason. One could be puzzled, amused, or perhaps even annoyed by this well-known pejorative image of the "wild" Balkans,[4] but – although not crucial for initiating the BHS – the feuilleton nicely serves as a) an example *par excellence* for popular perception and presentation of (violence in) the Balkans and b) a constant reminder of the kind of data, analyses, and findings required for (dis)proving such stereotypes. Because in the end, in reality, as well as in the cited feuilleton, the actual occurrence of (lethal) violence in the Balkans might very well differ from our images, stereotypes, and expectations. Just as in the short story, our expectations of a "wild and violent" Balkan need not be met in reality, even though they might very well be based on solid initial information, like the bar violence in the story, or the higher homicide rates, when it comes to criminological research.

Reflecting on the Balkans as a region of violence, *Sundhaussen* concludes that there is no empirical proof for a disposition to violence specific to the Balkans, just as there is no proof for some sort of "atavistic" hate between its different ethnic population groups. The differences are that in some societies, the rules for restraining violence, as well as the control mechanisms enforcing them, are simply less deeply rooted than in other societies (p. 20). This seems to be the case in the Balkans and clearly a long-term consequence of the region's historical, legal, and cultural legacy, rather than its inhabitants' collective "atavistic" or violence prone traits (p. 20).

3.1.2   The Balkans as a Historical Space Sui Generis

The Balkans, according to *Sundhaussen*, constitute a unique historical and cultural region of Europe or a sub-region of Southeast Europe, as they exhibit a cluster of characteristics that exist nowhere else in that particular concentration and combination (p. 9). The region's history from the end of the sixth century onward (great migration of the Slavs) can be divided into three main periods: 1. the period of the Byzantine Empire and the medieval Balkan states whose culture and civilization were shaped by the "Byzantine model"; 2. the 400–500-year

---

[3] Slivovitz is a fruit brandy made from damson plums and a very typical strong alcoholic drink throughout Southeastern Europe, produced both commercially and very frequently also privately.
[4] See Fn. 2.

period of direct or indirect Ottoman rule; 3. the period of modern state and nation building since the beginning of the nineteenth century to the present (p. 9). Obviously, in terms of structurally formative and long-term impact, the Byzantine legacy (including the medieval Balkan legacy) and the Ottoman legacy emerge as crucial regional traits.[5] While the North became predominantly Catholic, the South was predominantly influenced by the Orthodox Church and, in parts, has been reshaped by Islam (p. 7).

The Balkans are thus a textbook example of a region of migration and displacement – the conglomeration created by migrations within an area that is smaller than France proved to be a hornets' nest with regard to modern state and nation building (p. 16). Between 1875 and 1999, the Balkan region was as a whole or partly involved in a total of 12 wars, in which, besides the regular military, paramilitary units played a significant role (p. 18). These paramilitary units were associated with the tradition of "Hajduks" and "Klephts," the "outlaws" during the Ottoman period. While Balkan narratives honor them as "heroes," "warriors against feudal injustice," or "champions of national liberation," Ottoman sources denote them simply as "robbers." Undisputedly, "banditry" was a regional mass phenomenon from the seventeenth century onward, and in many respects, one could argue that it has remained one to this day,[6] entailing an enormous potential for insecurity and dissatisfaction (p. 18).

There is obvious continuity of this "banditry" as a mass phenomenon and historical legacy of the Ottoman Empire. But looking at its causes, rather than the phenomenon itself, according to *Sundhaussen*, the continuity consists of the fact that the Balkan states and their neighbors have not (yet) come to terms with their own history, whereas established Balkan "values" still remain unchallenged (p. 19). Since such setting impacts the societies of the whole region, not only the Balkans, but

---

[5] In this context it is necessary to briefly explain why, according to *Sundhaussen*, Slovenia and Croatia are not to be considered part of the Balkans. Although both Slovenia and Croatia did belong to the first and second Yugoslavian states, this period of 72 years was in historical perspective far too short to smooth out the differences toward the actual Balkan states (p. 6). For centuries, modern Slovenia was part of the Austrian crown land (and historically belongs neither to the Balkans nor to Southeast Europe), whereas Croatia and the Vojvodina were part of the Hungarian part of the Habsburg monarchy (and belong to Southeast Europe, but not to the Balkans), while the Balkan region was part of the Ottoman Empire for 400–500 years. The history of their religion, culture, civilization, and law took other paths than did the regions in the South, in the Balkans. Although the borders of the former multiethnic empires, the Ottoman and the Habsburg Empires, disappeared between the beginning of the nineteenth century and the end of WWI (not to mention the borders of the Eastern Roman/Byzantine Empire), they still surface as "phantom borders" in varying contexts (p. 7). Yugoslavia united very different regions within its borders under the "leitmotif" of the concepts of lingual kinship and the "family of nations," even though the members of the "family" had lived for centuries in completely different political, societal, economic, and cultural contexts (p. 7).

[6] Nowadays such "banditry" is referred to as criminal state capture or criminal tycoonization. The countries of the Balkan region show clear elements of such state capture, which includes links to organized crime and corruption at all levels of government and administration, as well as a strong entanglement of public and private interests (European Commission, 2018, p. 3). See also Pejić (2019) and Perry & Keil (2018) and the 2018 special issue 42/1 of Southeastern Europe on criminal state capture or etiologically very insightful Richter & Wunsch (2020).

likewise Southeast Europe, from a criminological standpoint, it is clearly justified to speak of a criminological space *sui generis*. Its particularities shape as much the region's criminal landscape, as they mold its criminal justice system, and more generally speaking public administration, as well as private business and the "way we get things done," here, in our part of Europe.

3.1.3 The Balkans as a Legal and Cultural Region

With respect to the legal cultures, following *Sundhaussen*'s findings, pre-modern Southeast Europe can be roughly divided into a Western Roman (Northern) and an Eastern Roman subarea, whereby the split of Christianity was pivotal for this division (p. 10). Until well into the nineteenth century, there existed an almost unmanageable plethora of legal systems that had either loose or no relationships with each other at all, with varying jurisdictional purviews, or that were interchanged repeatedly over the course of centuries (p. 10). Since they were often unsystematic, many of these legal systems in fact cannot be characterized as legal *systems* at all (p. 10). The unification and "Europeanization" of law in the Balkan states and the Romanian principalities developed in the course of the nineteenth century and have lasted to the present (p. 14). This process encountered major resistance by large parts of the population and representatives of a historic legal doctrine, who rejected the Roman legal system as "alien" and "artificial" (p. 14). The popular trust in laws and jurisprudence was correspondingly so minimal that many resorted to the protection of patronage networks, which in turn further eroded the already fragile legal quasi-system (p. 14).

Now, this widespread reliance on patronage networks, rather than state authorities and institutions, is not only deeply rooted in the historical, legal, and cultural tradition of the Balkans, but it is also largely present in the Balkans, as well as Southeast Europe, even nowadays. Neither the collapse of the socialist regimes in 1989 nor the southeastern enlargement process of the European Union, accompanied by the transposition of its *acquis communautaire* throughout the region, has managed to significantly impact this patronage legacy. Throughout Southeast Europe, especially the Balkans, personal and family or clan-like patronage networks in fact bundle up into a loosely interconnected web of relationships (referred to as *connections*) which almost completely mimic formal state structures and functions. In light of the briefly sketched legal, cultural, and historical legacy of the region, it should therefore come as no surprise that corruption, nepotism, and clientelism are present on a pandemic scale and generally considered good custom, rather than deviating from the norm. In the context of the BHS, it will be particularly interesting to see whether such broad reliance on patronage networks somehow impacts the occurrence or handling of (lethal) violence. Namely, formal state structures and functions in essence provide for the non-violent resolution of interpersonal conflicts and offer legit access to countless services. Now, if instead of relying on formal state structures and services, major parts of the population resort to patronage networks for settling their affairs and informal mechanisms of conflict resolution, one might immediately jump to the conclusion that this could perhaps explain the

Balkan-violence-paradox (Chap. 1). Whether this actually might be the case or not will be further discussed based on the first findings of the BHS (Chap. 6).

3.2   Criminological Research Setting

After having roughly sketched the region's historical, legal, and cultural legacy with regard to those *general* features deemed most relevant for understanding crime and (lethal) violence in its overall social context (Sect. 3.1), this section provides insight into more *specific* characteristics that describe and explain the criminological research setting the BHS has been conducted in. Whereas the general features were intended to portray the regional context necessary for understanding and explaining the *BHS findings*, the more specific features presented here are intended to illuminate the "who" and the "how" of the *BHS as a practical challenge*. The "who" deals with the current state of art in criminology in Southeast Europe and discusses essentials about what is currently going on in criminological research. The "how" deals with both the "how" of research funding and implementation and the "how" of gaining access to criminologically relevant data and the criminal justice system. In essence, this section brings more color to the presentation of the BHS research design and its operationalization (Chap. 4). It transparently depicts all those challenges and benefits of conducting research that commonly remain well hidden in academic publications, although they are crucial for the critical assessment of any study and the value of its findings.

3.2.1   *Criminology in Southeastern Europe*[7]

Looking at the regional criminological setting, the first questions that emerge are "who is doing criminology?" and "what kind of research can be found?" Now, considering that criminology as a discipline is rather young, this question clearly deals more with the present time and less with the past. Nevertheless, one needs to stress that the very beginnings of criminology throughout the region had been interrupted by the post-Yugoslavian wars of 1991–1999. But even prior to that criminological research was significantly influenced by a socialist take on crime as a "Western" or "capitalist" sickness, against which the "brotherhood and unity" of the region was proclaimed to be immune. The few pockets of criminological research throughout the region that nevertheless existed could be found in Slovenia, Croatia, Serbia, and Macedonia. In the process of the violent dissolution of Yugoslavia, most of the existing criminological relations between these few actors were interrupted, and until rather recently one could not speak of an actual regional criminological community.

---

[7] For an in-depth regional analysis, see Getoš Kalac (2014); for country specific analysis on criminology and crime in Albania, Bosnia and Herzegovina, Bulgaria, Croatia, Greece, Hungary, Italy, Kosovo, Macedonia, Montenegro, Romania, Serbia, Slovenia, and Turkey, see the relevant country studies in Getoš Kalac et al. (2014), pp. 77–397.

Today in the 2020s, criminology in Southeastern Europe has been revitalized and has by far outgrown its initial few research locations (Meško, 2018). This is in part a consequence of a global rise in criminology's attractiveness, and it is also to be attributed to several visionary criminological key figures, first and foremost *Hans-Jörg Albrecht, Uglješa Zvekić,* and *Gorazd Meško,* who raised a new generation of criminologists and have been vigorously supporting their work throughout the region. In sharp contrast to the situation only a decade ago, today there is a highly productive and stable criminological community in Southeastern Europe, with at least one engaged criminologist in each of the region's states. Together they form the Balkan Criminology Network and have successfully revived and upgraded criminological research throughout the region (Meško, 2018). An interesting feature of these new Balkan criminologists is that, with a few exceptions, most of them have not undergone formal training/education in criminology, but instead have a background in (criminal) law, criminalistics, security studies, (social) pedagogy, sociology, psychology, social work, or former "defectology" (nowadays educational rehabilitation or special pedagogy). In many instances, they acquired criminological knowledge and skills through learning by doing, in the meaning that they simply started participating in regional and/or international criminological research projects[8] and in due process picked up the necessary knowledge and skills. Now, this is rather important to note, since such picking up of criminological craftmanship along the way of doing research bares the risk of being inferior to formal and structured criminological training/education, while it may also impact the likeness of mistakes and the capacity to handle all the challenges inherent to empirical research.

To sum up, the current criminological research community in the Balkans and relevant neighboring states can best be described as a small (with few exceptions in Slovenia, Croatia, Serbia, and Bosnia and Herzegovina) but yet highly productive network of a new generation of young researchers, who got "criminologized" along the way of conducting research, who are less concerned with the region's past than with its present and future, who operate with scarce if any institutional support in terms of funding, administration, staffing, logistics, or research tools, and who have in less than a decade become extremely engaged in European and global criminology. Due to the relatively small size of the criminological community, that only exceptionally counts more than two or three "criminologists" per country, many criminological topics have not been addressed (yet).[9] Nevertheless, as a fist major breakthrough, the region has managed to comprehensively "map" its criminological, victimological, and penological landscape and thereby strongly positioned itself within the European and global criminological community.[10] Before discussing common regional challenges that determine the research setting, it can be

---

[8] For instance: The International Self-Report Delinquency Study (Bezić, 2020), the European Sourcebook of Crime and Criminal Justice Statistics, the BHS, etc.

[9] So, for example, also homicide research within the framework of the European Homicide Research Group (Liem & Pridemore, 2012).

[10] This "mapping exercise" has been generously funded by the Max Planck Society and been made possible through the support of the Max Planck Institute for Foreign and International Criminal Law. The relevant book trilogy is part of the Balkan Criminology publication series and covers general criminology (Getoš Kalac et al., 2014) and victimology (Meško et al., 2020), with penology forthcoming.

concluded that criminology in Southeastern Europe, especially the Balkans, despite numerous impressive achievements in the past decade, is still largely lacking behind criminology as practiced in the rest of Europe, as is well reflected by the regional lack of resources, knowhow, empirical research, higher education programs, institutions, and domestic as well as international publications.

3.2.2   The "Balkan Way" of Funding Research

Empirical research is usually rather costly in terms of resources. So, naturally when analyzing any given research setting, one should know some basic facts and figures about R&D funds and how these are made available to the research community. Looking at Southeastern Europe, the gross domestic expenditure on R&D in 2017 as share of the GDP was highest in Slovenia (slightly less than 2%), Hungary (slightly less than 1.5%), and Greece (slightly more than 1%), followed by Turkey, Serbia, Croatia, and Bulgaria (not even 1%), and Romania, North Macedonia, Montenegro, and Bosnia and Herzegovina (less than 0.5%) (Eurostat, 2019). This is well below the European average of 2% and a major indication of what the regional research setting in terms of funds and resources might look like.

Clearly, research funds are scarce, but this alone does not make the region an isolated case in its European context. In my observation, it is the clustering of further characteristics – like poor salaries of researchers and professors, limited or no access to publications, software (e.g., SPSS), research staff and equipment, with no or poor travel budgets for attending conferences – that sets the region apart from the rest of Europe. There is also an evident lack of privately funded research opportunities (e.g., national foundations), little if any support or incentives for publishing in leading international journals or managing projects, and lack of institutional capacity to apply for or manage domestic/European/international research projects. Finally, throughout the region, I notice an academic mentality that still largely thinks about research funding in terms of socialist and communist dimensions, meaning that everyone should by default get some basic funds, regardless of any kind of competitive criteria. Now, to this last point on mentality, one needs to add that this has been slowly changing. However, since public research funds are so sparse, whereas key gatekeepers commonly still belong to the old guard, a recognizable "Balkan way" of funding research throughout Southeastern Europe has developed. In my experience this, "Balkan way" heavily relies on patronage networks and may well be depicted as a special type of *(criminal) tycoonization* of public research funds.[11]

---

[11] The term (criminal) tycoonization denotes the process of (criminally or mysteriously) acquiring exceptional wealth, power, and influence by individuals or interest groups. In Southeastern Europe, it is used with an extremely negative connotation due to the shady/criminal privatization process of public resources and war profiteering which have led to an unexplainable accumulation of wealth and influence by entrepreneurs (Getoš Kalac, 2021).

Bureaucracy has meanwhile inflated academia worldwide, including research and its funding (Martin, 2016; Nehring, 2016; Glaser, 2015). This issue inevitably touches upon the ongoing discussion on academic capitalism globally (Münch, 2016; Slaughter & Rhoades, 2004), but even more in transitional societies, like those found in the Balkans. Here, in the Balkans, with an established legacy of patronage networks, where corruption meets criminal state capture and dictates daily public and private business, one must seriously doubt that the sector of public research funding might somehow miraculously prove to be immune to its (criminal) tycoonization. Such immunity appears to be as likely as bureaucrats' or academics' overall immunity to deviant behavior, misconduct, corruption, or, for that matter, any kind of criminal behavior at all. Reliance on personal and family or clan-like patronage networks is a common feature throughout academia as it is in any other professional sector in Southeastern Europe (Getoš Kalac, 2021). But due to the fact that the overall funds these networks accumulate are extremely modest compared to other sectors of public expenditure, the public and scientific interest in the subject matter is accordingly low or nonexistent.[12] As discussed in the following paragraphs, the "Balkan way" in this context basically means that overly bureaucracy (in academia as well as in any other public sectors) is regularly being used (systematically) to limit access to funds and resources, which can also be seen as a regional legacy, whereas it is commonly the personal or academic and family or clan-like patronage networks that actually decide over (non)funding and resources, thereby (in)directly also determining research priorities and topics.

3.2.3   Criminal Justice Systems of the Balkans

As explained earlier in the context of the region's legal history and its legacy (Sect. 3.1), many of the Balkans' legal systems are in fact no *systems* at all. The current legal transposition of the European Union's *acquis communautaire* throughout Southeastern Europe in many ways resembles the legal "Europeanization" and unification process that took off back in the nineteenth century. The region's patronage legacy and culture of working around the official system, rather than through the system, although clearly undermining the rule of law principle and breeding corruption on a pandemic scale, should not simply be dismissed as negative phenomena. They are a given fact and yet another *specificum* of the region. Instead of providing for judgmental outrage and listing the countless harmful impacts of this regional condition, my following observations rather focus on explaining how the *system* actually works. The purpose is to shed some light on the "how" of the BHS not only in terms of data access and research operationalization but also in terms of contextualization of its findings.

In sharp contrast to most of criminal justice systems in the rest of Europe, those in Southeastern Europe, particularly in the Balkans, operate quite informally. While writing a research data access request in Germany or Sweden (probably implying the usage of a purposively designed online form) would be the first step in accessing criminal justice data, in Southeastern Europe, this would in fact commonly be the

---

[12] For an exception, see Institut društvenih znanosti Ivo Pilar (2018) and Getoš Kalac (2021).

last step to take. First and foremost, one uses his/her patronage network, be it a personal, family, or clan-like one, in order to identify the relevant gatekeeper whose blessing or support would be needed to gain access. Then, again using one's patronage network, the gatekeeper is approached informally and kindly asked for or bluntly pressured into granting access. This step is repeated until mastered or alternative gatekeepers can be identified. After access has informally be granted, usually as a last step, a research data access request is handed in. Now, obviously if one's patronage network includes such gatekeepers, all the previous steps are skipped and access is achieved instantly, most likely even without retroactively handing in a pro forma written request.

Although this "working around the official system" might seem highly problematic from the aspect of equality, in many ways the system operates quite similar to the "working through the official system" in other parts of Europe (e.g., Germany or Sweden). The only striking difference is that in Southeastern Europe (data access) success commonly depends on personal, family, and clan-like relations, whereas in most of the rest of Europe, the outcome is usually determined by professional or institutional influence and reputation, which is grounded in proven competences and achievements. In light of this, one could argue that both systems are equally unfair, with the only difference being that this unfairness in the Balkans is a result of personal chance or luck, whereas in most of the rest of Europe, it is a result of professional work and institutional achievements. The Balkan "system" as simplistically sketched above applies throughout the (criminal) justice system as well, ranging from staffing and advancement, all the way to launching criminal investigations (or rather not). Now, the unsuccessfulness of rooting out such practices in Southeastern Europe cannot simply be explained by the legacy of patronage networks. It is more likely explainable by a synergy of such a legacy, the patronage networks acting as a perpetuum mobile and the necessity of doing favors in order to be able to call in favors, which are an indispensable resource to work the system. So, as a conclusion, perhaps even a lesson and a takeaway, any researcher interested in conducting criminological adventures throughout the Balkans should be prepared to invest time and energy into personal networks, equip himself/herself with ample patients, and beware that it is customary to (first) get things done informally – commonly over food and drinks.

References

Bezić, R. (2020). *Juvenile delinquency in the Balkans: A regional comparative analysis based on the ISRD3-study findings*. Berlin: Duncker & Humblot.

European Commission. (2018). *A credible enlargement perspective for and enhanced EU engagement with the Western Balkans*. COM (2018) 65 final, 6 Feb 2018. Strasbourg.

Eurostat. (2019). Gross domestic expenditure on R&D, 2007 and 2017 (%, relative to GDP), 16 Sept 2019.

Getoš, A. M. (2012). *Politische Gewalt auf dem Balkan. Schwerpunkt: Terrorismus und Hasskriminalität – Konzepte, Entwicklungen und Analysen*. Berlin: Duncker & Humblot.

Getoš Kalac, A. M. (2021). (Cyber) bullying by faceless bureaucracy in research funding: A case study from the Balkans. In R. Haferkamp, M. Kilchling, J. Kinzig, D. Oberwittler, & G. Wößner (Eds.), *Unterwegs in Kriminologie und Strafrecht – Exploring the world of crime and criminology. Festschrift für Hans-Jörg Albrecht zum 70. Geburtstag* (pp. 511–540). Berlin: Duncker & Humblot. Extended preprint retrievable from https://www.bib.irb.hr/1054936. Accessed 20 Jan 2021

Getoš Kalac, A. M. (2014). Mapping the criminological landscape of the Balkans. In A.-M. Getoš Kalac, H.-J. Albrecht, & M. Kilchling (Eds.), *Mapping the criminological landscape of the Balkans: A survey on criminology and crime with an expedition into the criminal landscape of the Balkans* (pp. 23–55). Berlin: Duncker & Humblot.

Getoš Kalac, A.-M., Albrecht, H.-J., & Kilchling, M. (Eds.). (2014). *Mapping the criminological landscape of the Balkans: A survey on criminology and crime with an expedition into the criminal landscape of the Balkans*. Berlin: Duncker & Humblot.

Glaser, E. (2015). Bureaucracy: why won't scholars break their paper chains?. *Times Higher Education*, www.timeshighereducation.com › features › 2020256.article 2 Oct 2020.

Institut društvenih znanosti Ivo Pilar. (2018). Kamo ide hrvatski znanstvenoistraživački sustav: prema racionalnoj reformi ili prema entropiji i urušavanju? Zagreb, www.pilar.hr/wp-content/uploads/2018/03/Izvjesce.pdf. Accessed 2 Oct 2020.

Liem, M. C. A., & Pridemore, W. A. (Eds.). (2012). *Handbook of European homicide research: Patterns, explanations, and country studies*. New York: Springer.

Martin, B. R. (2016). What's happening to our universities? *Prometheus, 34*(1), 7–24.

Meško, G. (2018). Before going to Sarajevo: A revival of comparative criminology in the Balkans. *Newsletter of the European Society of Criminology, 16*(3), 2–3.

Meško, G., Sárik, E., & Getoš Kalac, A. M. (Eds.). (2020). *Mapping the Victimological landscape of the Balkans: A regional study on victimology and victim protection with a critical analysis of current victim policies*. Berlin: Duncker & Humblot.

Möller-Kaya, T. (2016). Illustration 'Die Stunde des Sliwowitz'. *Lufthansa Magazin, 1*, 48.

Münch, R. (2016). Academic capitalism. *Oxford Research Encyclopedia of Politics*, https://oxfordre.com/politics/view/10.1093/acrefore/9780190228637.001.0001/acrefore-9780190228637-e-15. Accessed 2 Oct 2020.

Nehring, D. (2016). The deskilled academic: Bureaucracy defeats scholarship. *Social science space*, www.socialsciencespace.com/2016/02/the-deskilled-academic-bureaucracy-defeats-scholarship/. Accessed 2 Oct 2020.

Pejić, J. (2019). *All Western Balkan countries need "Priebe Reports" to measure state capture.* European Western Balkans – Centre for Contemporary Politics, 8 Feb 2019. Belgrade; https://europeanwesternbalkans.com/2019/02/08/priebe-report-state-capture-western-balkans/

Perry, V., & Keil, S. (2018). The business of state capture in the Western Balkans: An introduction. *Southeastern Europe, 42*(1), 1–14.

Richter, S., & Wunsch, N. (2020). Money, power, glory: The linkages between EU conditionality and state capture in the Western Balkans. *Journal of European Public Policy, 27*(1), 41–62.

Slaughter, S., & Rhoades, G. (2004). *Academic capitalism and the new economy: Markets, state, and higher education*. Baltimore: Johns Hopkins University Press.

Sundhaussen, H. (2014). The Balkan Peninsula: A historical region *Sui Generis*. In A.-M. Getoš Kalac, H.-J. Albrecht, & M. Kilchling (Eds.), *Mapping the criminological landscape of the Balkans: A survey on criminology and crime with an expedition into the criminal landscape of the Balkans* (pp. 3–22). Berlin: Duncker & Humblot.

Timmerberg, H. (2016). Die Stunde des Sliwowitz. *Lufthansa Magazin, 1*, 48.

Chapter 4
The Balkan Homicide Study: Research Design and Operationalization

Abstract This chapter provides indispensable insights into the BHS research design and its practical operationalization. The chapter's leitmotiv is that there is no perfect empirical violence research – with each study we come a bit closer to revealing few of the many unknowns of (lethal) violence, while making valuable mistakes that open new lines of research. In that sense, the most meaningful way of handling the methodological and practical imperfections of the BHS is to be transparent and objective about the crucial "whys and hows" of its research design. After explaining the study's two core objectives, the main methodological decisions and challenges will be presented. This includes various aspects of designing and using a unique instrument for data collection, sampling strategies, data representativeness, normative and statistical context, as well as field work and data analysis challenges. The chapter's aim is to realistically depict all the methodological ups and downs of the BHS. It will equip readers with all the necessary information needed to arrive at own, potentially even divergent, conclusions on the study's first findings.

Keywords BHS violence typology · Case analysis · BHS sample characteristics · Representativeness · Normative context analyses

After having provided an overall analysis of the state of art in European homicide research and its balkanization (Chap. 2), as well as the necessary Balkan-specific context and research setting (Chap. 3), we now turn to the specific methodological context the BHS findings are imbedded in. The broad scientific and cultural context enables one to understand the necessity and value of the BHS as a criminological research undertaking. The specific context allows for an informed and critical consumption of the study's data, its findings, as well as their interpretation and the first conclusions these lead to. Section 4.1 presents the study's core objectives, whereas Section 4.2 deals with the main methodological aspects of the BHS. Section 4.3 contains essential sample features and provides the normative and statistical context relevant for assessing the representativeness of the survey's sample. Section 4.4 discusses the key practical aspects of the BHS field work in light of their potential impact on the completeness and quality of the collected data.

© The Author(s) 2021   35
A.-M. Getoš Kalac, *Violence in the Balkans*, SpringerBriefs in Criminology,
https://doi.org/10.1007/978-3-030-74494-6_4

4.1   Objectives

The BHS has two core objectives which simultaneously follow two separate lines of research. The first one deals with the social and normative construction of violence, whereas the second one investigates the empirical realities of violence in the Balkans.

4.1.1   Social Construction of Violence

How is violence socially constructed and normatively perceived? Is there a common normative understanding of violence throughout the region or are there considerable national differences? Who has the power to define violence and how is this reflected throughout the criminal justice process? Are there detectable factors that might help explain or even predict the outcome of such a definitional process? These are the lead questions we had in mind when designing the first line of inquiry for the BHS. In order to answer them, we collected a vast amount of procedural data within the case file analysis (Sect. 5.4).

Empirical data collection on procedural aspects proved to be rather challenging. Since the BHS aims at investigating the power to define violence (Chap. 1), it was clear from the very onset that it needs to cover not only those incidents that are finally adjudicated as (lethal) violence by courts but also all incidents initially defined as (lethal) violence by police and/or prosecution that consequently got redefined throughout the criminal justice process (and potentially dropped out). Ideally the BHS would therefore have tracked all relevant incidents from the police stage throughout the prosecution stage and eventually up to the court stage. However, based on prior experience, access to police files was assessed as extremely unlikely in all of the participating countries, whereas even the access to prosecution files proved extremely challenging in some of the countries. The first findings on the normative, hence social construction of violence, are presented in Sect. 5.4, although it has to be noted that many questions remain unanswered in terms of understanding the process of defining and redefining (lethal) violence.

Due to lack of access to police and prosecution files, it is not possible to comprehensively assess the power to define violence on the side of the police, as accomplished in prior violence studies (Sessar, 1981; Hess, 2010; Dölling, 2015). But even with these prior studies, caution is required, as there is solid empirical evidence on a considerable *dark figure of homicides* that remain undetected by medical doctors or pathologists, due to their incorrect initial classification of actual homicides as natural (unsuspicious) deaths. Estimates go as high as 1200 for such undetected homicides annually in Germany (Universität Rostock, 2017; Esanum, 2017) and 175 to 350 additional homicides per year in the Netherlands (Bijleveld & Smit, 2006, p. 196). European homicide research has only recently started to investigate the flow of homicide cases through the health and justice systems (Liem & Eisner, 2020; Liem, 2018), marking a valuable new line of research the BHS will also need to consider prospectively.

4.1.2   Empirical Realities of Violence

The BHS's second line of research focuses on the three mainstream questions commonly addressed by violence research: What are the (situational) characteristics of the incidents (Sect. 5.1)? Who are the offenders (Sect. 5.2)? Who are the victims (Sect. 5.3)? This obviously involves the victim-offender relationship, as well as the relationship between co-offenders and co-victims and numerous contextual aspects of the incident. The BHS is also interested in finding out what (lethal) violence in the Balkans actually looks like, particularly with the aim of understanding the *Balkan-violence-paradox* (Chap. 1) and empirically challenging the violent Balkan stereotype (Sect. 3.1).

The BHS objective is thus to detect possible protective traits in victims that survived violent incidents. This is achieved by searching for deescalating situational factors that might be useful in preventing lethal violence and by investigating potential violent traits in the offenders, as well as accelerators of deadly situations (Chap. 6). Due to these objectives, the BHS focuses on attempted homicides as well as completed ones, especially since there is said to be evidence that the characteristics of offenders of attempted homicides might be markedly different from those of completed homicide offenders.[1] Subsequently, it is reasonable to presume that the characteristics of attempted homicide victims might be markedly different from those of completed homicide victims as well. However, with regard to (lethal) violence, the BHS data analysis will clearly distinguish between attempted and completed homicides, unless indicated otherwise. Eventually, the BHS's first findings will provide for a first look at the empirical realities of (lethal) violence in the Balkans, in line with the BHS violence typology used for classifying all analyzed incidents according to the type of violence (situation and context), victim-offender relationship, motive, as well as particularly cruel, sexual, and affective perpetration (Fig. 4.1).

4.2   Methodology

The following paragraphs deal with the basics of BHS's methodology. This includes a description of why and how the case file analysis was conducted, an explanation of the study's instrument, a discussion of the BHS violence typology, and concluding remarks on cautiousness regarding BHS data.

---

[1] *Smit* et al. (2012, p. 18) argue that there obviously is a huge difference between attempted and completed homicides. They refer to Bijleveld and Smit (2006) as an example of prior research which shows that (in the Netherlands) the characteristics of offenders of attempted homicides were found to be markedly different from those of completed homicide offenders. Yet, *Bijleveld* and *Smit* (2006, p. 199) clearly state that due to pragmatic and conceptual reasons, only completed homicides were the object of their study. Eventually neither Bijleveld and Smit (2006) nor *Smit* et al. (2012, p. 18) provide empirical justification for excluding attempted homicides nor do they elaborate on the actual characteristics of offenders that are said to be "markedly different" or explain why attempted homicides might constitute a "criminologically distinct phenomenon."

4.2.1   Case File Analysis

In the region, studies on (special types of) violence cannot be conducted from official statistics such as those published by the national statistical authorities,[2] but have to be tailored to the questions at hand and thus need special data collection efforts. That is why the BHS was from its onset designed as a case analysis-based study. This also made particular sense in light of the fact that lethal violence is a rather rare criminal occurrence throughout the region,[3] while homicides may be generally considered only the "tip of the iceberg" of underlying crime (Liem in Chap. 2). As such it might best be investigated and captured by focusing in depth on a smaller and more recent sample, instead of looking at long-term trends or more general statistical data, which would by default block out the necessary level of incident details. Thus, looking at the BHS objectives, case analysis appeared to be the only meaningful research method able to collect most of the relevant data. Surely, one could have applied a mixed method approach and combined case analysis with, for example, media analysis of reports on (lethal) violence, interviews with criminal justice practitioners, and a broad variety of other methods, but this was simply not within the BHS's resources in terms of funds, scope, staff, or time. The study is original as much as it is explorative in nature since little, if any comparable, research exists in the region. It marks a solid starting ground for future research, which based on first BHS findings, will hopefully be able to look more specifically into various different features of (lethal) violence in the Balkans.

4.2.2   Research Instrument

At a very early stage of designing the BHS, it became clear that none of the countries will grant access to police case files. Therefore, the BHS is based on court and prosecution case files, in which the available information has been validated, but which (compared to police files) contain no information on unsolved homicides, drop-out cases that did not lead to a prosecutorial investigation (e.g., due to lack of evidence or unknown offender), or initial (attempted) homicides that were redefined as other types of violence (e.g., grave bodily injury with lethal consequence) by the prosecution. This focus on court and prosecution files is well reflected in the BHS questionnaire that was used for data extraction from the files, especially in terms of its overall structure and the type of variables. The starting point for the BHS questionnaire was a questionnaire designed and tested by *Hans-Jörg Albrecht* for the study of violence in Uruguay, which investigated the level of violence related to cannabis trade and how the cannabis market may lead to insecurity, all in the context

---

[2] For an excellent overview of official crime and criminal justice statistics in the Balkans, see UNODC, 2010.

[3] Looking at the most recently publicly available ESB data (European Sourcebook Group, 2011), we conclude that homicides make up between 0.04 and 0.27% of all registered crime in 2011 in those BHS countries for which data has been collected (Croatia: 0.27%; N. Macedonia: 0.16%; Slovenia: 0.04%; Hungary: 0.26%; Romania: N.A.; Kosovo: N.A.).

of the Uruguayan model of cannabis legalization (CORDIS, 2017). This questionnaire was extensively broadened at the first study meeting by the initial BHS partners and thus adopted to the specific regional context. In hindsight, it would have been immensely helpful and surely much easier to simply adopt some or even all of the variables from prior homicide studies, as well.[4] However, this became evident only after the field work had already been conducted and is partly also a consequence of the "learning by doing" approach throughout the region (Sect. 3.2).

The questionnaire itself is divided into five main parts covering procedural variables, case variables, offender variables, victim variables, a descriptive case summary, and relationship variables which include two variable subsets: the victim-offender and victim-victim relationship (BHS Codebook, 2021). In total, the BHS questionnaire contains more than 200 variables and a descriptive case summary, while the BHS database in fact comprises five separate databases due to the different counting units the variables relate to (case, offender, victim, victim-offender relationship, and victim-victim relationship). The coding was done by the BC office and the Violence Research Lab in Zagreb and partly assisted by the MPICC's criminology department in Freiburg. In terms of the questionnaire length and complexity, one might very well describe it as an extremely impressive challenge, or more frankly speaking, as a practical and analytical nightmare. Depending on the court or prosecution case file complexity and "thickness," as well as the national researcher's proficiency in case analysis and the level of legal expertise, data collection per case lasted from approximately 30 minutes to 1 hour and 15 minutes, or on average for approximately 45 minutes.

The BHS was conducted in English language, meaning that both the questionnaire used during data collection (except for Romania) and the input language are in English (including Romania).[5] Although this minimized potential errors inherent to back and forth translation of English language questionnaires to/from different languages, it is safe to assume that the English language aspect had a minor impact on the interpretation of some variables during data collection.[6] In order to minimize the language impact and to consolidate the understanding of all the variables regardless of the normative differences in all the BHS countries, a special BHS workshop was held in November 2017. During this workshop, a data collection manual was jointly drafted. It in detail explained all the terms used in the questionnaire. This step was

---

[4] Initial contacts to the European Homicide Monitor (EHM) and one of its lead researchers *Marieke Liem* had been made in an early stage of the BHS, but due to time and staff constraints, neither the BHS instrument could be adjusted to the EHM nor were particular variables from the EHM adopted to the BHS instrument. Coordination with comparable studies and validated instruments has meanwhile been achieved and should not only upgrade BHS's future methodology and data analysis but also enable the EHM to significantly broaden its scope toward Southeastern Europe. For more detail on the EHM, see Liem et al., 2013 or Liem & Pridemore, 2012 and Liem in Chapter 2.

[5] For Romania, the language used for collection of data via the questionnaire was Romanian due to the assessed low English language proficiency of the national field researchers. All data collected via the questionnaires (in Romanian language) was then transferred into the database and in doing so translated into English language where relevant, for example the short case descriptions.

[6] E.g., blood feud was occasionally interpreted as violence between blood relatives. The term conflict (prior to the incident) could be understood either broad or narrow, ranging from a verbal argument all the way to a physical hassle.

also necessary because partners from some of the initially selected BHS countries could not participate in the study after all, so partners from other countries stepped in and needed to get acquainted with the study and its methodology. The workshop was also attended by a high-ranking prosecutor from the region who provided valuable expert insights on the type and quality of data contained in case files as well as research questions that would be particularly valuable to criminal justice practitioners.

As basis for the methodological finetuning of the questionnaire during this workshop in November 2017, the Croatian pilot study was used. Again, as a consequence of a hands-on learning approach, the Croatian pilot study was in fact the Croatian BHS study conducted in 2016 and 2017 on a full national sample "gone wrong." This became clear only after the data collection was already completed (paper & pencil style), and all of the data were entered into statistical databases. During data cleaning and preliminary analysis, we found that some crucial variables were missing in the questionnaire, and a considerable share of cases was surveyed unobjectively by one of the field researchers. Hence, the first BHS data collection in Croatia became the BHS pilot study and the BHS questionnaire was significantly improved before repeating the whole exercise in Croatia and starting data collection in the remaining BHS countries.

4.2.3   BHS Violence Typology

After the successful completion of data collection in six countries, all BHS partners, except for Kosovo, delivered their statistical databases to the BC office in Zagreb. For Kosovo, the filled out paper questionnaires were delivered and data entry into statistical databases was conducted by BC staff. Data cleaning was conducted centrally by the BC office in Zagreb for all the databases and consecutively by two researchers. In the end, the BHS databases in their questionnaire-like form proved to be utterly user-unfriendly, even user-hostile, and successfully evaded any meaningful attempt for analysis. In a nutshell, due to having used a new research instrument and several counting units without beforehand having designed elaborate pathways for later-on data analysis, the BHS databases proved to be far too complex for meaningful analysis. So, for example, in order to identify cases of intimate partner violence and analyze these in terms of gender or age of the offender and the victim and the *modus operandi*, the relevant relationship variable from the victim-offender database was needed. However, the relationship databases (victim-offender, offender-offender, victim-victim) displayed a huge share of missing data on the one side, whereas, on the other side, the combining of the relationship variables with the relevant variables from the case-, offender- and victim databases simply proved to be too demanding and time-consuming. So, although the data needed for such kind of analysis was clearly contained in different databases, we did not manage to extract all the necessary variables and combine them correctly and meaningfully.

Many sleepless nights down the road were spent puzzling about a sensible solution. Having read through all the descriptive case summaries in an attempt to get at least a general sense about "what's in there," sheer despair led to the idea of an emerging BHS violence typology. Basically, by using the case descriptions (or when these were missing or incomplete by using specific variables to reconstruct the descriptions), a new set of key variables was constructed. Using these key variables, all cases were classified according to the type of violent incident, victim-offender relationship, and motive, as well as particularly cruel, sexual, and affective perpetration. This proved to be not only very user-friendly with respect to data analysis but also in line with the fact that the BHS does not work from a specific theoretical perspective nor does it aim for testing any specific theory on (lethal) violence.

Essentially being an exploratory study, the BHS was in itself designed to start from no theoretical base assumption. So, what better way is there than by taking what you have and after having looked at it in full detail to classify all of it into sensible larger categories/types. Instead of trying to fit all cases into predefined categories based on empirically weak or unfounded prior assumptions or prior research from other parts of the world, the collected data from the actual incidents was used as the basis for developing a corresponding typology – the BHS violence typology (Fig. 4.1, BHS Typology, 2021). Methodologically speaking, the tailor-fit development of a study-specific violence typology that is in fact rooted in the study's own data appears far sounder and more appropriate, than using any other hypothetical typology, particularly in light of lacking prior research or data on (lethal) violence in the region.

As the BHS violence typology shows (Fig. 4.1), only 3.6% of all cases were excluded from the overall sample due to not being a (lethal) violent incident at all (mainly false reports). In only 1.5% of all violence cases, the incident was perpetrated in a cruel manner, whereas in only 2.1%, there was a sexual component involved in the incident. In as much as 40.1% of all violence cases, the incident was categorized as an affective (non-premeditated) act of (lethal) violence. Incidents were categorized as affective if the offender acted impulsively and timely closely connected to a prior dispute or conflict with the victim without having had the time or opportunity to "cool down" or plan the violence beforehand. The share of 40.1% affective violence cases simultaneously means that the remaining 59.9% of cases are premeditated.

Looking at the type of violence (context and situation), as much as 36.7% of cases were *other private violence*[7] compared to 26.1% of *other public violence*[8] and

---

[7] This type denotes incidents that take place in a private setting, usually at home, with only the victim and the offender present. This type was selected only if none of the more specific types applied (e.g., infanticide, which commonly also takes place in a private setting, but it is a more specific type of violence than private violence). The "privateness" or intimacy of this type's setting indicates that the victim should feel safe and might likely be off-guard, while the offender has more control over unwarranted interruptions by other persons or potential witnesses.

[8] The idea is to identify all incidents that occur in a public setting and are not in some other way more specified regarding location (bar violence), motive (robbery), or context (hooliganism). The main characteristic of this type of violence is the lack of "privateness" or intimacy characterizing private violence, in order to distinguish between, for example, an offender killing his son after a heated argument in a park and an offender killing a stranger in a supermarket. The publicness or

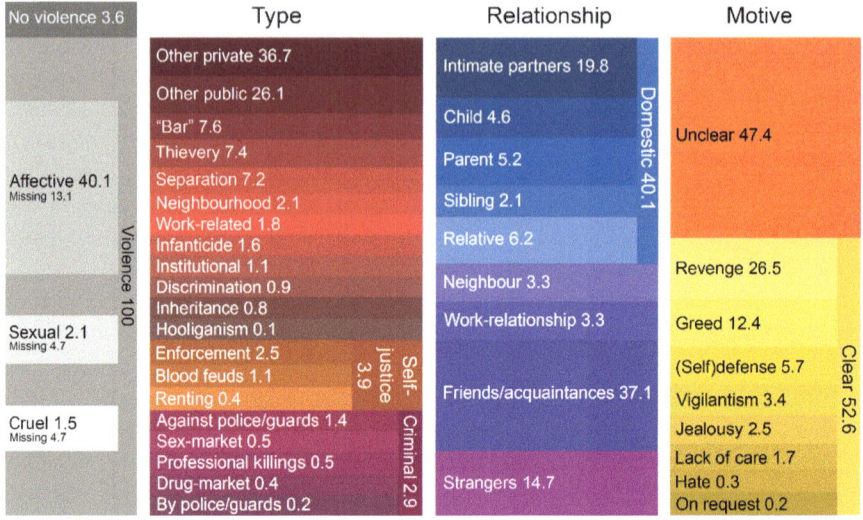

Fig. 4.1 BHS Violence Typology with shares of subcategories within each category ($N_{violence}$ 1997; counting unit: case; 0.1% missing data for type; 1.6% missing data for relationship; 0% missing data for motive); for more detail, see BHS Typology 2021

only 7.6% of *bar violence*[9]. The remaining two most frequent types were *thievery violence*[10] with a share of 7.4% and 7.2% of *separation violence*[11]. Even after combining the remaining types of violence into larger categories (3.9% of *self-justice*

---

openness of the setting indicates that the victim should feel less safe and be more on guard, while the offender has less control over unwarranted interruptions by others or potential witnesses.

[9] The main characteristic of this type of violence implies a larger group of people in a "party atmosphere" which (usually) includes alcohol consumption, fun, and a generally relaxed leisure setting. Although commonly committed in a regular (night) bar, *bar violence* might also be committed at a home party or a street fair, or in any other location where the same atmosphere is present. If the incident takes place in front of/at the parking lot of a nightclub, it is also considered as this type, since the situational context remains the same. However, the mere location of the incident is not enough for determining this type of violence (e.g., the offender and the victim have an argument over a money debt while drinking in a bar and the offender kills the victim – the money debt makes this case more specific; hence, it is a case of *enforcement violence*, despite being located in a bar).

[10] This type is characterized by the context and setting of trying/gaining financial profit through thievery. These cases usually pertain to robbery, burglary, or theft "gone wrong." The context of illegally gaining financial profit can be found either on the side of the offender or on the side of the victim, the latter indicating that the person being robbed might end up being the actual offender with regard to the violent incident, whereas the case motive would be (self)defense. The decision to combine robbery, burglary, and theft "gone wrong" within *thievery violence* is based on the finding that the difference between robbery, burglary, and theft cases cannot be determined clearly enough based on collected case file information. Basically, consistency and accuracy of "typing" were chosen over the "specialty" of the three different offenses, since all three unquestionably are *thievery* in nature when it comes to context and setting.

[11] The main criterion for this type of violence is the offender's dissatisfaction over the fact that his/her intimate relationship is ending or has ended. The main focus is on the "being broken up with." Thereby, the relationship between the victim and the offender is irrelevant – the context and setting

violence or 2.9% *of crime-related violence*), none of them made up a comparably large share as the previously listed five types. On a methodological note, it needs to be stressed that other private and other public types of violence due to lack of more detailed or conclusive information in the case descriptions could not be classified as any of the phenomenologically more specific types. This basically means that within this share of 62.8% of all cases, an unknown distribution of more specific violence types remains hidden.

In terms of the victim-offender relationship (focusing on the status of the victim toward the offender) of (lethal) violence, only 14.7% of incidents can be classified as *stranger violence*, whereas as much as 40.1% of all cases are *domestic violence* cases. This finding is in line with findings from previous studies which show that commonly in Europe (Liem & Pridemore, 2012), as well as in the United states (Timrots & Rand, 1987; Riedel, 1987), the vast majority of (lethal) violence relates to non-stranger violence, not to stranger violence.[12] The finding also makes sense with regard to the rather low levels of (violent) street crime in the Balkans (UNODC, 2008), since one would expect a much higher share of stranger violence in case of a higher prevalence of (violent) street crime in the Balkans (e.g., more robbery gone wrong cases). It needs to be highlighted that the BHS stranger category does not include those cases in which the relationship was unknown, but only those cases in which data indicated that the victim-offender relationship was one between strangers. The same applies for all the BHS violence typology categories – lack of data needed for clear categorization was categorized as missing data.

Returning to the victim-offender relationship and in light of the high share of domestic (lethal) violence cases, it will be interesting to take a closer look at this type of victim-offender relationship, particularly related to violence between intimate partners (19.8%). The same goes for (lethal) violence between friends and acquaintances (37.1%). The BHS violence typology distinguishes not only between the typical three broad categories of victim-offender relationships (intimates, acquaintances, and strangers), but also in much more detail captures the different degrees of intimacy between the victim(s) and the offender(s). Therefore, it will be possible to investigate this feature of (lethal) violence in much more detail. The BHS typology enables not only the testing of different variables connected to the victim-offender relationship but also allows for analyzing relevant motives and types of violence (Chap. 5).

Focusing on the motive of the offender, in almost half of the cases (47.4%), this remains *unclear*,[13] since the BHS violence typology applies a very restrictive

---

are decisive, meaning that the victim of separation violence is not only the offender's (former) intimate partner but may also be the new or a previous partner.

[12] For constructive criticism of the traditional concept of *stranger violence* and empirically founded suggestions for improvement, see Polk, 1993.

[13] *Unclear* motive was assigned to a case whenever it was highly speculative to determine one of the following motives *clearly*: revenge, greed, (self)defense, vigilantism, jealousy, lack of due

classification approach. It assigns (apparent, not actual) motive to a case only if this is rather straight forward. Such a restrictive approach is grounded on the fact that the exact determination of human motive *ex post facto* and based solemnly on case files, as well as its methodological construction in form of a variable, is highly dubious (at best). But even in the case of "determined," motive cautiousness is requested, since this is merely an *apparent motive*, not the *actual motive*, which in essence is only known to the offender, although even this intrinsic insight gets extorted by processes such as neutralization. Out of the clear motives, approximately half of them are *revenge*[14] (or 26.5% of all cases) and one-quarter is *greed*[15] (or 12.4% of all cases). As the next chapter will demonstrate, the BHS violence typology allows not only a meaningful data analysis but also enables to test the soundness of the briefly presented typology itself, by cross-checking the violence types with victim-offender relationships and violence motives, as well as numerous other BHS variables.

4.2.4   Cautious Use of BHS Typology and Data

The BHS violence typology was developed by analyzing and "typing" each case on the basis of its descriptive case summary and its relevant variables according to actual violence, violence type, victim-offender relationship, motive, as well as cruel, sexual, and affective perpetration. In the next step, all these initial different case types were combined into phenomenologically meaningful broader categories, up to the point where further broadening of the categories (new variables) would have led to losing the phenomenological specifics of the category itself. All "typing" and "categorizing" decisions were noted and the final typology was validated by an external researcher with a non-legal social science background who was not involved in the BHS or any of the "typing" and "categorizing" of cases, using only the descriptive case summaries and the written typology instructions (BHS Typology 2021).

---

care, hate, or on request. Unclear motive was also assigned when it was not clear which single one of multiple motives is the dominant one or when the case involved too many offenders and/or victims to clearly identify one single main motive.

[14] *Revenge* denotes a motive directed toward getting even with the victim for some kind of wrong that has been committed toward the offender. It is irrelevant whether "the wrong" is essentially banal in its nature or even occurred at all – the *perception of the offender* that he/she is being the "victim" of some sort of injustice is decisive. Revenge in some instances might seem to overlap with *(self)defense*, but the difference is that revenge is assigned when "the wrong" against the offender was not a criminal offense/misdemeanor, but rather something more banal (e.g., victim spilled a drink on the offender in a bar). The situation is similar with regard to *vigilantism*.

[15] The offender is motivated by acquiring financial gain (e.g., money, drugs, land, and car) from his/her actions, risking that by doing so he/she might harm someone. In cases such as debt collecting, if the offender is the debtor, the motive is *greed* since his/her main goal is to *keep* the money that is not rightfully his/hers. While contrary, if the offender is the creditor, he/she is motivated by *revenge* because his/her main goal is to *retrieve* something that is rightfully his/hers.

The highest variance in classification decisions relates to the categories motive (19%),[16] type of violence (16%)[17], and affective perpetration (13%)[18]. This result should come as no surprise. The variables motive, type, and affective are very tricky and highly sensitive constructs in terms of methodology, and thus realistically difficult to exactly determine, even if one witnesses a violent incident, let alone conducts the categorization based on case files or only descriptive case summaries. The remaining categories display a variance of less than 10% (violence: 1%; sexual: 0.6%;[19] cruelty: 2.6%;[20] relationship 8.4%). The overall 91.3% match in classifying the BHS cases is more than enough to justify a preliminary validation of the BHS violence typology as a methodologically sound and well-functioning analytical tool. Nevertheless, caution is needed with regard to both typology and data due to the "second-hand" nature of the source of data (case files), potential interpretation effects of researchers collecting the data (from the case files), and likely interpretation effects of researchers analyzing the descriptive case summaries. Thus, with regard to motive, type, and affectivity of the (lethal) violence incidents, caution is advisable, even though the BHS typology applies a very restrictive approach.

The presented violence typology (Fig. 4.1), although aiming at highest possible phenomenological accuracy, primarily targets methodological consistency and clarity with regard to its classification criteria. This basically means that in case of the two aims conflicting, the typology opts for consistency and clarity of classification criteria, instead of capturing all phenomenological details, which are rather noted as missing data/unclear, than forcefully speculated into most likely categories. That is why the BHS violence typology is not to be understood as a general typology of (lethal) violence, but as a study-specific typology designed to capture, analyze, and present the study's first findings in a meaningful manner.

With regard to having introduced a new research instrument (despite its pilot-testing on a full national sample, as well as its foundation in a previously used instrument), cautiousness is clearly in place. Thus, as with any comparable (lethal) violence survey based on case file analyses, cautiousness is advisable with regard to the aforementioned problem of a presumably significant dark figure of (lethal) violence. The same applies with respect to missing data, missing case files, as well as substantive and procedural criminal law differences between the different BHS

---

[16] The variance largely relates to a more frequent usage of the category "unclear motive" and also indicates differentiation problems between the categories "vigilantism" and "revenge."

[17] The variance can mostly be explained as a tendency to rather use the broader categories (e.g., other public or other private) than the more specific ones (e.g., honor killings and blood feuds, discrimination, separation, or neighborhood). In that sense, the classification is not incorrect, but rather less specific.

[18] If including variation caused by more frequent 999 entries (unable to determine due to lack of information), instead of 0 entries (no), the share of different classifications is 23%. This essentially means that the independent validator was less likely to exclude the possibility that the incident might have been perpetrated in an affective manner.

[19] Same explanation as provided in Fn. 18 applies accordingly, with a resulting variance of 6%.

[20] Same explanation as provided in Fn. 18 applies, with variance in 8% of cases.

countries, but even within the same countries, due to normative changes (offense descriptions as well as sentencing ranges) over time. Due to its relevance for the study at hand, the missing data issue will be explored in more detail in Chapter 5 and in view of the different BHS counting units (see also Appendix). Finally, it needs to be stressed that neither statistical nor normative context analyses were possible for Kosovo, due to lack of data.

4.3   Sample

This section will briefly describe the BHS sample, including information on the study's main sampling decisions regarding covered time period, included/excluded offenses (Table 4.1), and scope of sampling within each country, for example, full national or regional sample (Table 4.3). In order to assess the study's representativeness, Eurostat data on officially registered completed homicide suspects is compared to corresponding BHS data (Fig. 4.2). In order to assess the potential impact of the country-specific normative frameworks, relevant context data and analyses of national substantive criminal law provisions will be presented as well (Table 4.2). This section will be concluding with an overview of basic data collection features and main BHS sample characteristics (Table 4.3). More detailed descriptive analysis with particular focus on lethal and non-lethal violence will then be presented in Chap. 5.

4.3.1   Sampling

Due to being interested in the current features of (lethal) violence throughout the region, the BHS strived for a cross-sectional sample of finally adjudicated cases – a snapshot of more recent (lethal) violence in the Balkans. Therefore, the BHS covers all cases that were finally concluded at the prosecution stage and/or court level within a recent five-year period (except for N. Macedonia and Hungary with a three-year period): 2010–2014 (Croatia), 2011–2016 (Romania), 2011–2015 (Kosovo), 2013–2015 (N. Macedonia), 2010–2014 (Slovenia), and 2012–2016 (Hungary). Except for Romania, where we opted for a regional sample due to country size/population and anticipated case load, the BHS aimed for a full national sample, in order to reach a target sample size of approximately 600 cases per country. Those countries with smaller populations (as expected) don't even come close to this sample size, but this would have been different if the initially agreed BHS countries could have been covered (Albania, Bosnia and Herzegovina, Serbia, and Turkey).

Now, in terms of comparability of the collected data and ensuring that the BHS covers only those recent (lethal) violence incidents that had been committed (not finally concluded) in the targeted five-year period, we should have sourced case files according to the year the incident took place, not the year of final decision. This was however practically not feasible, since it would have implied that the registry clerks at all prosecution offices and/or courts pick out all the relevant cases by the year the offense was committed (in most countries this information is not even noted in the registries) and then out of these select only those that have been finally concluded, as case file analysis of ongoing proceedings was not possible. Due to this, the BHS sample includes (lethal) violence incidents dating back as far as 1986.

With regard to criminal offenses included, the BHS covers a broad range of (lethal) violence incidents summarized under the categories basic, privileged, and qualified homicide (Table 4.2), whereby it focuses exclusively on adult offenders. The decision to exclude cases involving juvenile offenders was based on practical reasons (difficult access to juvenile courts' case files), while balancing costs and benefits of including such cases in the sample (e.g., additional courts to cover for a very small number of cases). In the majority of BHS countries, the source of the case files (prosecution or court) corresponds to the stage of the criminal proceedings at which the case had been finally concluded (Table 4.3, column titled *stage*). However, in those instances when court case files could not be accessed or access to prosecution case files was simply far more convenient, case files were (also) sourced from the prosecution, but are in fact a "copy" of the concluded court case file kept in the prosecution's records (including data on the final outcome of the case). The field work for the BHS was largely conducted during 2018, except for the Croatian pilot study which mainly took place throughout 2017.

4.3.2   Statistical Context: BHS Representativeness

In order to assess how representative the BHS sample is with regard to officially recorded incidents of (lethal) violence in each of the covered countries, it was necessary to make more than only one compromise. The main question is which data from the BHS sample should be compared to which data and from what other (most relevant/reliable) source. Due to having included in the BHS sample attempts as well as negligent homicides and keeping in mind the considerable methodological differences in (attempted) homicide definitions even among relevant international sources (Smit 2012, p. 15), as well as in all six official national sources of homicide data, the answer to the aforementioned question is indeed complex and would deserve its own chapter.

In a nutshell, after having analyzed several national and international sources of homicide data and their methodologies, Eurostat data proved to be most suitable and thus available for five out of the six countries (Kosovo excluded). In terms of counting unit, the offender is used, and with regard to matching definitions of homicides, the BHS sample has been reduced to include only completed homicides, while the Eurostat count includes by default all of the following: murder, honor killings, serious assaults leading to death, death as a result of terrorist activities, dowry-related killings, femicide, infanticide, voluntary manslaughter, extrajudicial killings, and killings caused by excessive use of force by law enforcement/state officials. The years refer in both instances to the year in which the suspected offender was reported to the police (BHS) and thereby was counted as a suspect (Eurostat). Now, obviously the assessment of the BHS sample's representativeness has clear limitations, and it thus varies from one country to another due to targeted sample size and country population size, which explains the lower representativeness for Romania (where only a regional sample was collected) and extremely high representativeness for Slovenia (Fig. 4.2).

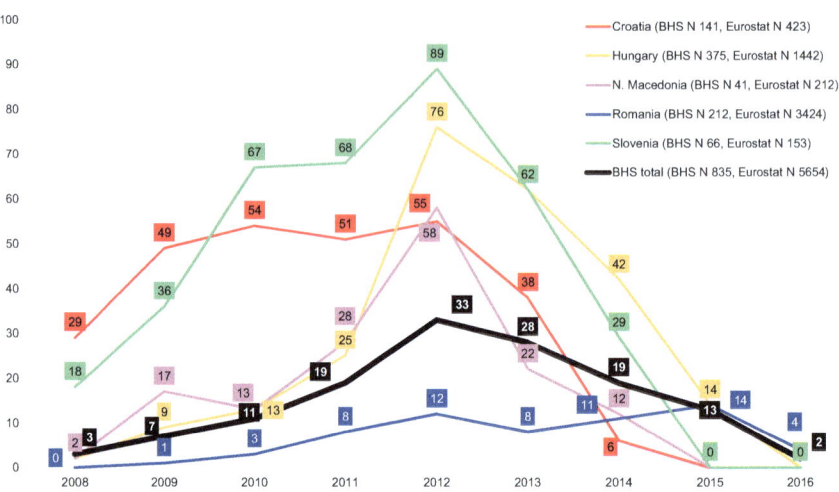

Fig. 4.2 BHS representativeness for BHS suspected homicide offenders as share of Eurostat suspected homicide offenders between 2008 and 2016

For the years 2011, 2012, 2013, and 2014, we observe that the total BHS sample is most representative. For 2012, the BHS sample covers one-third of all homicide suspects in five BHS countries as reported to Eurostat. Bearing in mind that the BHS is a casefile-based study aiming at a first snapshot of (lethal) violence in the selected countries, this is quite an achievement of its own. Even more if one considers that the overall representativeness of the total BHS sample as analyzed for Fig. 4.2 is under a considerable influence of the Romanian sample, or to be more precise, under the influence of Romania's population size, case load and the fact that a regional, not a national sample was obtained. If one were to exclude the Romanian sample, then the representativeness of the remaining 4-country BHS sample would amount to as much as 70% for 2012. Considering the BHS's explorative nature, as well as the far broader definition of homicide applied by Eurostat (which also includes serious assaults leading to death) and the impossibility to account for the representativeness of the overall BHS sample (including attempted homicides and the Kosovo sample), it is not possible to exactly assess the study's representativeness.[21] However, the assessment as presented here might very well be qualified as a "worst case scenario," or in other words present the lower range of the BHS's representativeness.

4.3.3   Normative Context: BHS Comparability

From a methodological perspective, the BHS's normative context is relevant not only with respect to sampling and offenses included/excluded (Table 4.1), but even more when it comes to data analysis and interpretation. First, there are the usual

---

[21] For full detail on Eurostat homicide classification methodology, see UNODC, 2015, p. 33.

Table 4.1 BHS definition of homicide in six participating countries[a]

	BHS	HR	HU	SI	MK	RO	XK
Attempts	✓	✓	✓	✓	✓	✓	–
Lethal assaults	X	X	X	X	X	X	–
Euthanasia	X	✓	X	X	✓	✓	–
Assistance with suicide	X	X	✓	X	X	✓	–
Infanticide	✓	✓	✓	✓	✓	✓	–
Dangerous driving	X	X	X	X	X	X	–
Abortion	X	X	X	X	X	X	–
Unintentional homicide	✓	✓	✓	✓	✓	✓	–
Lethal traffic offenses	X	X	X	X	X	X	–
Lethal sexual offenses	X	X	X	X	X	X	–
Lethal property offenses	X	X	X	X	X	X	–
Counting unit	Case		&	Offender		&	Victim

Legend: *HR* Croatia, *HU* Hungary, *SI* Slovenia, *MK* North Macedonia, *RO* Romania, *XK* Kosovo, ✓ yes, *X* no

[a]The classification purposely adopts the outline of a comparable classification applied by Smit et al. (2012) (p. 15) with regard to highlighting differences in four international sources of homicide statistics (United Nations Surveys on Crime Trends and the Operations of Criminal Justice Systems, Eurostat, European Sourcebook of Crime and Criminal Justice Statistics, World Health Organization), in order to enable comparison with BHS homicide definitions by country

methodological challenges inherent to all comparative research and data collection that is based on or sourced from different national criminal justice agencies. These challenges relate mainly to varying offense definitions as well as their varying sentencing ranges, on the one side, and to their changes over time, on the other side, meaning that not even within the same country, the offense definitions or the sentencing ranges need to be consistent. Now, the longer the time frame in which the sampled incidents took place, the more frequent the variations in the relevant normative contexts, and thus potentially more impactful their influence on the findings and their interpretation.

In case of the BHS, the longest time frame covered by the total BHS sample is 28 years (Table 4.3). Country-wise, we find the longest time frame covered for the Croatian BHS sample (25 years). During this time span, as many as four different penal codes were applicable in Croatia, not even counting all the in-between changes in single homicide-relevant criminal law provisions (definitions and/or sentencing ranges). In order to capture all the criminal law variations in the six BHS countries, while also considering these changes over time, a normative context analyses has been conducted. The main findings are presented in Table 4.2, whereby the sentencing ranges displayed provide the minimal and the maximal proscribed sentences throughout the entire period.[22]

The presented findings show the complexity of the normative framework the BHS findings are embedded in, just as much as they demonstrate the scope of variations in homicide-relevant offenses and sentencing ranges throughout the different countries. Clearly, not even the category of "basic" homicide is a clear overlap in all surveyed countries, with variations being even more noticeable in case of "qualified" and "privileged" homicide offenses, both with regard to homicide definitions and sentencing ranges. Looking at the total BHS sample, the possible sentencing outcomes range from 5 to 20 years for basic homicide, 10 years to life imprisonment for qualified homicide, 0.08 to 20 years for privileged homicide, and 0.5 to 15 years for negligent homicide. In methodological terms, one might argue that such normative findings call for weighting of the national sentencing variables in order to enable comparisons of sentences imposed on offenders. However, if one considers that it is not only the individual sentence that "measures" a societies reaction to (lethal) violence but also the sentencing framework provided by criminal law itself, then a weighting of the national sentencing variables would (unjustifiably) distort the findings. Nevertheless, further in-depth research into this matter would be highly feasible, as it is a fundamental question not only for the BHS but also virtually for all comparative criminological research works that are based on criminal justice data and/or sources from different countries.

---

[22] The normative analyses are limited to the special parts of the relevant national penal codes applied on the sampled incidents (offense definitions and sentencing ranges). If one would have included all the relevant provisions from all the applicable penal codes' general parts (e.g. concurrence, mitigation and remission of punishment, or the principle of *lex mitior* regarding the application of most lenient penal code), then for example in case of Croatia the death penalty as well as the maximum penalty of 50 years imprisonment would also need to be considered.

Table 4.2 Classification of homicides and sentencing ranges (in years) in six BHS countries

	Basic homicide	Sentence range	Qualified homicide	Sentence range	Privileged homicide	Sentence range	Negligent homicide	Sentence range
HR	Murder	5–20	Aggravated murder	10–40	Manslaughter, infanticide, killing on request	1–10 0.25–8 0.5–8	Negligent homicide	0.5–5
HU	Murder, aiding and abetting suicide of vulnerable person	5–15	Aggravated murder, infanticide	10–Life	Voluntary manslaughter	2–8	Negligent homicide	1–5
XK	Murder	–	–	–	–	–	–	–
MK	Murder	5–15	Aggravated murder	10–Life	Manslaughter, infanticide, murder (noble motives)	1–5 0.25–3 0.5–5	Negligent homicide	0.5–5
RO	Murder	10–20	Aggravated murder	10–Life	Infanticide, instigating or helping suicide, killing on request	1–7 1–20 1–5	Professional negligent homicide, negligent homicide	2–15 1–5
SI	Murder	5–15	Aggravated murder	15–30	Manslaughter, infanticide	1–10 0.08–3	Negligent homicide	0.5–5

Legend: *HR* Croatia, *HU* Hungary, *XK* Kosovo, *MK* North Macedonia, *RO* Romania, *SI* Slovenia

4.3.4 Sample Description

The BHS successfully sampled a total of 2073 (lethal) violence cases, which include a total of 2416 offenders and 2379 victims (excluding the pilot study). Out of these sampled cases and by using the BHS violence typology, a total of 1997 cases, including 2321 offenders and 2299 victims, were confirmed as actual cases of (lethal) violence. The total BHS dropout of 3.6% of sampled cases, involving 4.4% of offenders and 3.3% of victims, is a consequence of having sampled cases in the prosecution stage, which were finally concluded mainly as false reports and/or as dismissals (due to lack of evidence). Since there was no clear indication that these cases reflect actual incidents of (lethal) violence, they were not considered in the data analysis. The smallest sample sizes as expected relate to the smallest countries (Kosovo, N. Macedonia, and Slovenia), with Hungary, Romania, and Croatia all reaching the initially targeted sample size of approximately 600 cases. Basic data collection information and sample and BHS database characteristics are displayed in Table 4.3.

4.4 Field Work

Full disclosure and transparency on empirical research appear impossible in terms of methodology and research operationalization without providing at least a brief overview of the main features and misfortunes of the relevant field work. Notwithstanding the great overall success of the BHS, its modest resources, the quite challenging regional research setting, and limited prior experience in comparable empirical adventures on the side of most national partners are certainly some of the aspects of the field work that may have had an impact on the completeness and quality of the data. A first set of issues relate to the mainly voluntary engagement of the researchers conducting the case file analysis (paper & pencil style). These were mainly (PhD) students who got reimbursed for actual costs encountered due to their field work (travel and accommodation costs), while renumeration for their time/work was symbolic (if at all provided). In many instances, the completeness of the questionnaires and quality of data (especially the descriptive case summaries) depended on the interest and motivation of the single field researchers. Due to mainly having entered the data into statistical databases after the field work had already been conducted, there was only exceptionally a possibility to go back to the source case file for missing data or double-checking "strange" entries. Often times the success of field work also depended on the persistence and social skillfulness of the researchers on the spot, especially in those instances when access to court/prosecution case files was authorized by the relevant official in charge, but then denied or incomplete when showing up as agreed in the prosecutions'/courts' registries. Most data collection had to be conducted at the prosecution/court venues throughout each country, which put additional pressure on field researchers to be as quick as possible, particularly in those instances where registry clerks were not overly enthusiastic about the researchers' presence and the additional workload put on them by having to sort out (and put back) the requested case files.

Table 4.3 BHS data collection and main sample characteristics

Data collection			Sample						Database		
Country	Time	Stage	Cases	Offenders	Victims	Timeframe/period	Coverage	% Dropout of cases/offenders/victims	Cases	Offenders	Victims
HR pilot	2016–17	P., court	686	743	760	1981–2014/33	National	–	–	–	–
HR	2018	P., court	563	622	650	1989–2014/25	National	7.8/9.3/7.1	519	564	604
HU	2018	P., court	609	732	709	1994–2016/22	National	0.5/0.4/0.4	606	729	706
XK	2018	Court	74	104	97	2003–2012/9	National	1.4/1.0/1.0	73	103	96
MK	2017–18	Court	96	107	142	1997–2014/17	National	0/0/0	96	107	142
RO	2018–19	P., court	598	705	626	1997–2017/20	Regional	4.7/47/4.8	570	672	596
SI	2018	P., court	133	146	155	1999–2015/16	National	0/0/0	133	146	155
BHS	2016-19	P., court	2073	2416	2379	1989–2017/28		3.7/3.9/3.4	1997	2321	2299

Legend: P. prosecution; *Time* the year the field work has been conducted; *Stage* the level of final case conclusion; *Sample cases/offenders/victims* the number of cases/offenders/victims sampled and initially analyzed; *Timeframe/period* the years in which the oldest and most recent incidents covered by the BHS sample took place and the length of the covered period in years; *Coverage* indicates whether the sample is a full national one or partial/regional; *% dropout of cases/offenders/victims* indicates the share of cases/offenders/victims that was excluded from the BHS database due to lack of being incidents of (lethal) violence; *Database cases/offenders/victims* the number of cases/offenders/victims included in the final BHS database and eventually analyzed; HR Croatia; *HU* Hungary; *XK* Kosovo; *MK* North Macedonia; *RO* Romania; *SI* Slovenia

When it comes to interrater reliability, it must be mentioned that the Croatian BHS pilot study was a valuable experience that was shared with all BHS partners prior to their field work. In the pilot study, one of the field researchers consistently reinterpreted case file information from the perspective of the offender instead of collecting the information as documented in the case files. This was detected only after the whole data collection was completed and in the process of entering the data into the database. Based on this experience, all BHS partners were instructed to check the questionnaires periodically for "strange" entries. The vast majority of variables deals with factual information (e.g., dates, legal qualifications, weapons used, and sentence), so the effects of interrater reliability should be minimal in this regard. They are most likely to have had some impact on the short case descriptions and motives as initially covered by the questionnaire. However, tests or analyses checking the scope and possible impact of interrater reliability were not conducted. Since data cleaning and coding as well as classifying the cases in line with the BHS violence typology were conducted centrally at the BC office in Zagreb by two researchers, the impact of differences in ratings at this stage was minimized. Thus, the BHS violence typology ratings were checked independently by an external researcher not involved in the BHS or the designing of the typology – with a rather good result (Sect. 4.2).

Looking at the different BHS country samples, only for the Kosovo sample, additional cautiousness is advisable (see also Appendix). Thus, for Kosovo, the statistical and normative background analysis could not be conducted, and this was also the only country sample delivered to the BC office in Zagreb in paper-version, with limited feedback information from the national research partner.

In conclusion, would we have done the BHS field work differently looking back and could we have anticipated some of the misfortunes? Yes, of course. But would this have been possible within the given circumstances? No, clearly not, and even provided significantly more resources, experience, and staff, neither the completeness nor the quality of the collected data would have been significantly higher, since the majority of missing data is a consequence of the source case files' incompleteness and quality, which becomes most obvious when looking at the data in full detail (Chap. 5).

References

BHS Codebook. (2021). *The Balkan homicide study: Codebook*, www.balkan-criminology.eu/bhs-codebook/. Accessed 20 Jan 2021.

BHS Violence Typology. (2021). *The Balkan homicide study: Violence typology*, www.balkan-criminology.eu/bhs-typology/. Accessed 20 Jan 2021.

Bijleveld, C., & Smit, P. (2006). Homicide in the Netherlands: On the structuring of homicide typologies. *Homicide Studies, 10*(3), 195–219.

CORDIS. (2017). *Drug legalization of Cannabis in a developing Country*. The Uruguayan Model, https://cordis.europa.eu/project/id/627046/reporting. Accessed 9 Aug 2020.

Dölling, D. (2015). Zur Anwendung der Mordmerkmale in der Strafrechtspraxis. *Forensische Psychiatrie, Psychologie, Kriminologie, 9*(4), 228–235.

Esanum. (2017). *Studie zeigt große Mängel bei Leichenschau: Mit dem Messer im Rücken ins Krematorium?* 04.12.2017, www.esanum.de/today/posts/mediziner-fordern-bessere-leichenschau. Accessed 16 Sept 2020.

European Sourcebook Group. (2011). *SBK database* 5th ed_180222, https://wp.unil.ch/europeansourcebook/date-bases/5th-edition/. Accessed 01 Dec 2020.

Hess, A. (2010). *Erscheinungsformen und Strafverfolgung von Tötungsdelikten in Mecklenburg-Vorpommern.* Mönchengladbach: Forum-Verlag Godesberg.

Liem, M. (2018). The Flow of homicide through the system. *leidensecurityandglobalaffairsblog*, 02.07.2018, https://leidensecurityandglobalaffairs.nl/articles/the-flow-of-homicide-through-the-system. Accessed 13 Oct 2020.

Liem, M., & Eisner, M. (2020). Special issue: From homicide to imprisonment: Mapping and understanding the flow of homicide cases. *Homicide Studies, 24*(3), 207.

Liem, M., & Pridemore, W. A. (Eds.). (2012). *Handbook of European homicide research.* New York: Springer.

Liem, M., Ganpat, S., Granath, S., Hagstedt, J., Kivivuori, J., Lehti, M., & Nieuwbeerta, P. (2013). Homicide in Finland, the Netherlands, and Sweden: First findings from the European Homicide Monitor. *Homicide Studies, 17*(1), 75–95.

Polk, K. (1993). Observations on stranger homicide. *Journal of Criminal Justice, 21*(6), 573–582.

Riedel, M. (1987). Stranger violence: Perspectives, issues, and problems. *Journal of Criminal Law and Criminology, 78*(2), 223–258.

Sessar, K. (1981). *Rechtliche und soziale Prozesse einer Definition der Tötungskriminalität.* Freiburg/Breisgau: Max-Planck-Institut für Ausländisches und Internationales Strafrecht.

Smit, P. R., de Jong, R. R., & Bijleveld, C. C. J. H. (2012). Homicide data in Europe: Definitions, sources, and statistics. In M. Liem & W. Pridemore (Eds.), *Handbook of European homicide research* (pp. 5–23). Springer: New York.

Timrots, A. D., & Rand, M. R. (1987). *Violent crime by strangers and nonstrangers.* Bureau of Justice Statistics Special Report, http://www.ncjrs.gov/App/publications/abstract.aspx?ID=103702. Accessed 15 Oct 2020.

Universität Rostock. (2017). *Die meisten Todesbescheinigungen weisen Fehler auf: Studie der Uni Rostock bringt erschreckende Fakten ans Tageslicht,* 01.09.2017, http://www.uni-rostock.de/universitaet/kommunikation-und-aktuelles/medieninformationen/detailansicht/n/die-meisten-todesbescheinigungen-weisen-fehler-auf-16349/. Accessed 16 Sept 2020.

UNODC. (2008). *Crime and its impact on the Balkans and affected countries.* Vienna: UNODC, https://www.unodc.org/documents/Balkan_study.pdf. Accessed 14 Oct 2020.

UNODC. (2010). *Development of monitoring instruments for judicial and law enforcement institutions in the Western Balkans 2009–2011. Background research on systems and context - justice and home affairs statistics in the Western Balkans.* UNODC: Vienna, https://www.bib.irb.hr/513417/download/513417.CARDS_Background_Study_final.pdf. Accessed 13 Oct 2020.

UNODC. (2015). *International classification of crime for statistical purposes*, Version 1.0. Vienna: UNODC, https://www.unodc.org/documents/data-and-analysis/statistics/crime/ICCS/ICCS_English_2016_web.pdf. Accessed 12 Oct 2020.

Chapter 5
Violence in the Balkans: Regional Commons and Country Specifics

Abstract This chapter presents first findings from the BHS by providing data on main incident, offender, victim, and procedural characteristics of (lethal) violence in six countries of Southeastern Europe and the Balkans: Croatia, Hungary, Kosovo, North Macedonia, Romania, and Slovenia. The discussion will concentrate on regional commons, as well as country specifics with a particular focus on comparison between completed and attempted homicides. In terms of the type of violence, only the most relevant ones will be analyzed, whereby this relates to both the most prevalent and most interesting for the regional context. Thus, certain methodological aspects, like those related to missing data and the merging of datasets with different counting units, will be presented. Bearing in mind the overall scope of the BHS with more than 200 different variables, this chapter clearly presents but a fraction of all findings. Nevertheless, it is a solid starting point for future topic-wise more focused in-depth analyses, and will hopefully deliver food for thought on new lines of (lethal) violence and homicide research.

Keywords Missing data in violence research · Non-lethal violence vs. homicides · Violent incident characteristics · Victims of violence characteristics · Violent offender characteristics · (Lethal) violence prosecution

Taking into account the BHS's methodological context (Chap. 4) and its relevance for an informed and critical consumption of the study's data, in Sect. 5.1 main incident characteristics are presented. This is done by focusing on regional commons and country specifics, on the one hand, and with regard to commons and specifics of completed and attempted homicides, on the other hand. In Sect. 5.2, the main offender characteristics are presented, whereas in Sect. 5.3, victim characteristics, are discussed, both again focusing on regional commons and country specifics, thus contrasting completed and attempted homicides, or to be more exact, lethal and non-lethal violence. The BHS findings will also be discussed in view of prior homicide research findings.

Now, it is frequent in homicide research that only (completed) homicides are analyzed as one category, so for example in UNODC's Global Homicide Study (Global Study on Homicide, 2019) or the European Homicide Monitor. This makes

© The Author(s) 2021
A.-M. Getoš Kalac, *Violence in the Balkans*, SpringerBriefs in Criminology,
https://doi.org/10.1007/978-3-030-74494-6_5

sense from a pragmatic and practical, methodological, and even conceptual perspective, especially if homicides are considered to be essentially different phenomena than non-lethal violence (attempted homicides). However, the BHS takes a different approach and questions this assumption all together by presuming that there might be no essential difference in attempted and completed homicides, besides the obvious – the death of the victim. This perspective is partly rooted in a normative understanding of the concept of "attempt" in relation to homicide, which implies that the offender intended to kill the victim or negligently accepted the possibility of such an outcome and set in motion all necessary steps for this to occur, but that due to some event or action or pure luck, the victim did not die. Now, such normative perspective on "attempt" is clearly a consequence of the BHS being a case-file based study that sources its data from the criminal justice system which operates on the basis of normative constructs. By looking at the phenomenological features of attempted (non-lethal) and completed (lethal) homicide cases in the BHS sample, as we shall see throughout this chapter, first findings indicate that it might very well be a meaningful approach to look at attempted and completed homicide cases holistically, as one category or phenomenon.

While the first three sections of this chapter relate to the BHS's second line of inquiry about the criminological realities of (lethal) violence, Sect. 5.4 contains essential findings on how (lethal) violence is dealt with by the criminal justice system. This includes not only various procedural characteristics of criminal prosecutions and trials but also relevant outcomes and sentencing decisions. These findings relate to the BHS's first line of inquiry about the social and normative construction of (lethal) violence.

Now, the *missing data* challenge in homicide research is neither new nor unique to the BHS, and it would surely deserve a chapter of its own.[1] However, due to the condensed publication format, the missing data issue in the BHS will be briefly discussed at the outset of each section and limited to depicting the scope of missing data as relevant for each section. For a full overview of the scope of missing data by single variable and BHS country, see Appendix. If not indicated otherwise, the presented data excludes missing variables (dropping variables). Although such an approach clearly contains the risk of distorting results, by presenting the scope of the missing data problem transparently, it will at least be possible to objectively assess the magnitude of the potential result distortion. This then indicates the level of cautiousness with which the different results should be interpreted. Since there is no generally accepted rule of thumb when it comes to missing data from criminological case file analysis, one needs to make a critical assessment both on the scope of missing data and on the type of variable in question. Considering that "the only really good solution to the missing data problem is not to have any" (cit. Allison,

---

[1] See, for example, the 2004 thematic issue (3) of the *Homicide Studies* and, in particular, the overview provided by Riedel and Regoeczi (2004) or Liem in Chap. 2. Although the papers in the aforementioned special issue deal almost exclusively with the challenge of missing data in homicide research that is based on statistical datasets (not case file analysis), they provide a concise overview of the complexity and relevance of the issue at hand.

2002, p. 2), the sectional discussions of the BHS's missing data occurrences also aim at improving our understanding of how and why data is missing in case file analysis. In that sense, these discussions are as much a snapshot of lessons learned, as they are extremely valuable insights into the missing data phenomenon in case file-based violence research.

5.1   Incident Characteristics

While puzzling about (lethal) violence in the Balkans, one of the core questions we asked ourselves was "what kind of violence appears in this region of Europe?" This question has been triggered by what I deemed the *Balkan-violence-paradox* (Chap. 1). This paradox denotes a somewhat strange situation in which we notice higher homicide rates throughout Southeastern Europe in comparison to Central and Western Europe. At the same time, there is solid evidence that, compared to other parts of Europe, the Balkans do not fit the profile of a high crime region and appear to be much safer in terms of street and urban crime. Now, in terms of the BHS, this paradox should be reflected at least by rather low levels of crime-related (lethal) violence. The question at hand is, what other types of (lethal) violence seem to occur more frequently in the region, and how this might be explained?

5.1.1   Missing Incident Data

Analyzing the BHS's incident variables (counting unit: case), the scope of the missing data problem is mostly insignificant. The majority of variables display a share of less than 1–2% of missing data. The variables capturing a sexual connotation of the incident or cruel mode of perpetration display less than 5% of missing data, as do variables on the time of the incident. When classifying the incident as affective (non-premeditated), a more significant share of missing data appears (13%), as does in the case of determining the exact location in which the incident ended (20%). Interestingly, when it comes to the data on the location the incident started in, the misses are insignificant (0.3%). This might indicate that the data on the incident's ending location is not contained in the case files. Or that the variables distinguishing the incident's starting and ending location should be reconsidered, perhaps even be merged into one single variable in the future. For a full overview of the missingness in the BHS datasets, see Appendix.

A main initial concern for the BHS was the short case description variable. However, this has only 4% of missing entries (no case description at all), while approximately 25% of the case descriptions were of poor quality and needed to be supplemented manually by feeding in data from relevant other variables and databases (offender, victim, and victim-offender relationship database). With regard to distinguishing between completed and attempted homicides (as expected), there are no missing data. Nevertheless, as soon as one looks at the variables dealing with specific normative qualifications of the incidents, the missings increase significantly.

5.1.2   Attempted vs. Completed Homicides

Considering that an attempted crime (in legal terms, at least) means that the offender has taken all the steps necessary for the crime to be completed, it is quite dubious when homicide research relying on data sourced from the criminal justice system does not include attempted but only completed homicides. Clearly, there are valid pragmatic, practical, methodological, and even conceptual arguments in favor of such an approach, but at least the conceptual ones seem rather weak. The non-lethal outcome of a violent incident might be due to good or bad fortune of the victim, third-party intervention (or not), or a matter of the incident's micro-location. When discussing the matter of (lethal) injuries with forensic doctors, one quickly learns that an offender with a clear homicidal intent, aiming and shooting at the head of a victim, might thereby undeliberately cause only a flesh wound to the victim's neck, leaving the victim with a non-life-threatening injury and a scar. Another offender, lacking a homicidal intent, might aim and shoot at a victim's leg and, in case the bullet hits the leg's artery, undeliberately cause the victim's quick death. Neither conceptually, nor criminologically speaking, does it appear plausible or even justifiable to exclude the first scenario from a homicide study, based solemnly on the fact that the victim did not die (as intended).

Clearly, the question of a (non)lethal violent incident's "homicidality" is crucial for homicide research, and just as clearly neither strictly including nor strictly excluding all attempted homicides is the best solution. Perhaps we ought to think about "homicidality" more intensively in terms of varying degrees and sliding scales and less in terms of exact dichotomies like "attempted" and "completed" or "excluding" and "including." At least on first thought there seems to be no sensible reason for expecting a strikingly different incident constellation, or specific offender and victim profiles with regard to lethal and non-lethal homicidal violence. But even if there were, one would have to look at these cases of non-lethal violence and compare them to the lethal ones in order to be sure and identify potential differences, which is exactly what we will do in the next few paragraphs.

The BHS has analyzed 42% completed and 58% attempted homicide cases (N_{lethal} 847; $N_{non-lethal}$ 1150). Such an approximate 40/60 ratio of completed vs. attempted homicides in the total sample corresponds well to the country level in the case of Croatia (34/64; N_{lethal} 186; $N_{non-lethal}$ 333), Kosovo (36/64; N_{lethal} 26; $N_{non-lethal}$ 47), Romania (34/66; N_{lethal} 191; $N_{non-lethal}$ 379) and more or less Slovenia (45/55; N_{lethal} 60; $N_{non-lethal}$ 73), whereas it is inverted in case of North Macedonia (57/43; N_{lethal} 55; $N_{non-lethal}$ 41) and Hungary (54/46; N_{lethal} 329; $N_{non-lethal}$ 277) with more completed than attempted homicides. Due to no missing data on the competed-attempted variable and a quite comparable (or at least not dramatically different) ratio between completed and attempted homicides, the incident variables are analyzed with regard to the total sample in the next steps.

Bearing in mind the aforementioned 40/60 ratio of completed vs. attempted homicides, there are *no major differences* between completed and attempted homicides in the BHS sample when it comes to the distribution pattern of different characteristics within the following variables (Table 5.1):

Table 5.1 Similarities between completed and attempted homicides – distribution patterns of different characteristics within incident variables (counting unit: case; N 1997)[a]

Variable	Value	% Completed	% Attempted
Incident place (N$_{valid}$ 1,976)	rural	46.4	43.2
	urban	37.7	35.1
	capital	15.9	21.7
Incident location (N$_{valid}$ 1,994)	private	74.6	66.7
	public	25.4	33.3
Incident time (N$_{valid}$ 1,908)	evening	37.6	40.4
	afternoon	25.6	25.7
	night	21.8	20.8
	morning	15.0	13.1
Day of the week (N$_{valid}$ 1,994)	Monday	16.8	12.8
	Saturday	16.2	17.7
	Sunday	15.9	17.2
	Friday	15.6	13.8
	Wednesday	12.7	13.3
	Thursday	12.1	12.3
	Tuesday	10.8	13
Number of offenders (N$_{valid}$ 1,995)	one	87.8	90.2
	two	7.6	6.3
	three	3	2.3
	four or more	1.7	1.3
Number of victims (N$_{valid}$ 1,995)	one	90.4	88.9
	two	6.9	8.3
	three	1.8	1.9
	four or more	0.9	0.9
Sexual (N$_{valid}$ 1,903)	not sex-related	96	99.2
	sex-related	4	0.8
Cruel (N$_{valid}$ 1,904)	not cruel	96.6	99.7
	cruel	3.4	0.3
Affective (N$_{valid}$ 1,735)	premeditated	57.2	51.4
	affective	42.6	48.6
Main motive (N$_{valid}$ 1,997)	unclear	43.2	50.6
	revenge	25.3	27.4
	greed	16.9	9.0
	(self)defense	5.5	5.7
	vigilantism	3.7	3.2
Relationship (N$_{valid}$ 1,966)	non-stranger	88	82.8
	stranger	12	17.2

[a]The analysis does not compare the values of the shares as such due to the unequal share of attempted and completed homicides within the overall sample and due to the inverted ratio in the samples from North Macedonia and Hungary. Instead the analysis compares the distribution pattern of different characteristics within each variable differentiating between completed and attempted homicides. The results presented are based on valid cases as provided for each of the variables

We can observe that the distribution pattern of the different characteristics within each of the variables is the same for completed and attempted homicides (Table 5.1). Even in the case of the variable capturing the day of the week when the incident took place, we see that the distribution/frequency concentrates around the weekend. This is more evident for attempted than for completed homicides, where Saturdays and Sundays are the weekdays with the highest share of incidents. Looking at the completed homicides and their distribution throughout the days of the week, we notice that the concentration around the weekend is more dispersed and also includes Monday and Friday, whereby Monday probably reflects those incidents that took place in the night from Sunday to Monday. However, both completed and attempted homicides are clearly concentrated during/around the weekends. Even in cases of affective or premeditated violence, there appears no difference in the distribution pattern when comparing completed and attempted homicides. Most of all incidents, regardless of their lethality, are premeditated. Even in terms of the main motive, completed and attempted homicides in the BHS sample display an overlapping distribution pattern. Besides the category of unclear motive, which is the most common category for completed as well as attempted homicides, most frequent motives are in both instances revenge, greed, (self)defense, and vigilantism.

There are however *noticeable differences* between completed and attempted homicides observable in the BHS sample when looking at the characteristics of distribution pattern of incident within the variables victim-offender relationship and type of violence (Fig. 5.1). On first thought, one might assume that the variance in these variables could be under the influence of the incident's micro-location, indicating that homicides committed in a public location are simply more likely to remain attempted than those committed in a private location which more frequently result in the death of the victim. This assumption could not be confirmed based on the first cross-tabulation analysis, and it seems that the incident's micro-location is not an indicator for potential homicide lethality. More elaborate analyses would be needed to confirm these findings.

Clearly, it would be somewhat speculative to conclude at this point and without further in-depth analysis that there is a striking phenomenological difference between completed and attempted homicide incidents. However, the presented results (Table 5.1 and Fig. 5.1) also do not provide solid grounds for stating the opposite, meaning that there is an obvious difference between completed and attempted homicides (besides the obvious fact of the lethal consequence). Despite the results not being fully conclusive with regard to either of the two premises, they seem to be pointing toward the conclusion that (completed) homicides – *phenomenologically speaking* – might not be a special type of (lethal) violence. At least (completed) homicides in the BHS sample do not appear to be special enough to be studied outside the scope or even by completely disregarding attempted homicides. Now, if homicide research that focuses exclusively on completed homicide incidents is nevertheless considered legit and sound, then at least the same standard applies to homicide research that includes attempted homicides, especially when it comes to those variables that display no significant differences in distribution patterns in case of completed vs. attempted homicides (Table 5.1).

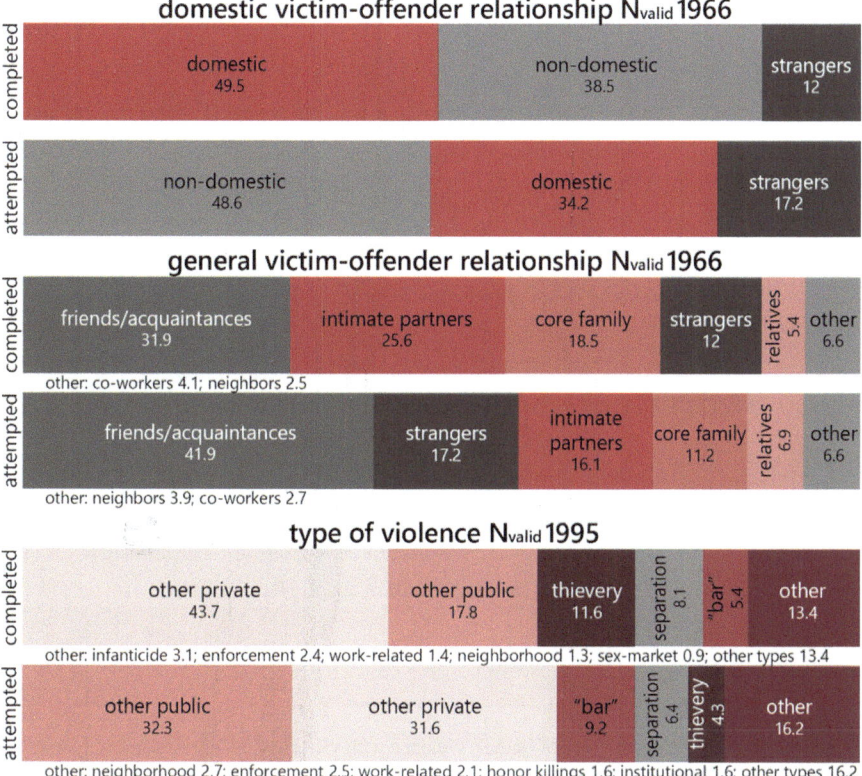

Fig. 5.1 Differences between completed and attempted homicides – distribution patterns of different characteristics within incident variables (counting unit: case; N 1997; in percentages)

5.1.3   Types of (Non)Lethal Violence

According to the BHS results presented above (Fig. 5.1), the five most frequent types of (non)lethal violence, including completed and attempted homicides, are displayed in the following figure (Fig. 5.2):

Although the distribution pattern of the different victim-offender relationships within the violence-type variable differs slightly – most noticeably in favor of private in case of completed and in favor of public in case of attempted homicides (Fig. 5.1) – clearly bar violence and thievery violence are not very frequent types of violence (Figs. 5.1 and 5.2). Neither are (lethal) violent incidents due to separation/divorce. Now, recalling the violent Balkan images and stereotypes (Sect. 3.1), this finding makes one wonder about their empirical justification. One would expect at least bar violence to occur much more frequently. Yet, this is not the case. Neither is it the case with regard to thievery (lethal) violence due to burglary, robbery, or theft. However, cautiousness is needed when it comes to such assessments, since incidents lacking phenomenological detail might have been classified as either other private or other public violence, which makes up a total of 62.9% of all cases.

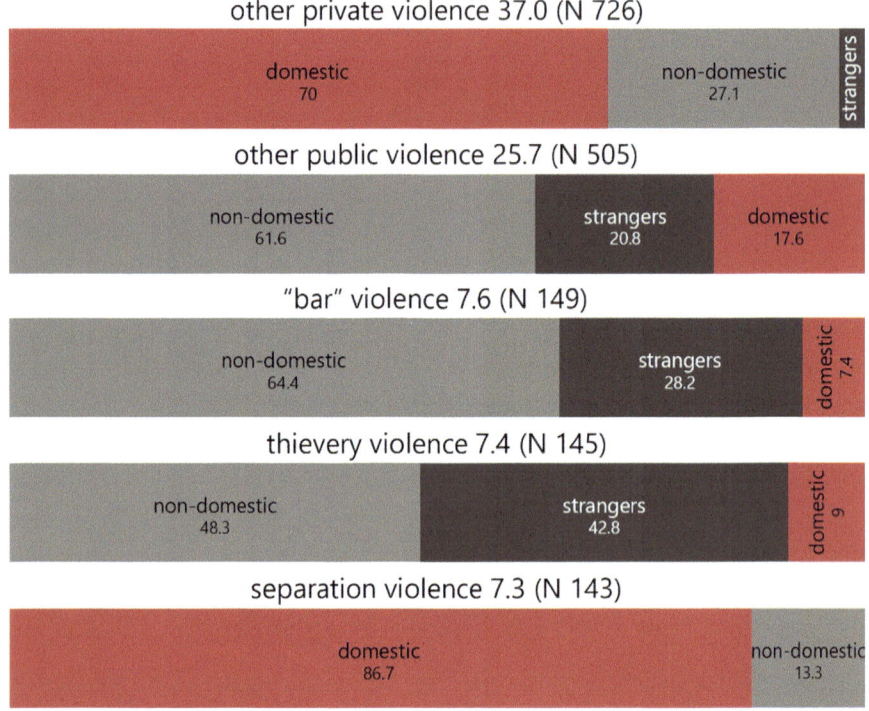

Fig. 5.2 Five most frequent types of (lethal) violence with victim-offender relationship (counting unit: case; N 1964; 1.7% missing data; in percentages)

Disregarding these two more general types of violence (N 1255) and focusing only on the phenomenologically much more specific types, the above/below shown distribution appears (Fig. 5.3).

It is almost impossible to assess to what extent such phenomenological distribution pattern of (lethal) violence according to the type of incident captures the realities of (lethal) violence or rather its normative constructions. It is possible that a significant share of bar and thievery violence, as well as any of the other types (both lethal, but even more non-lethal), were not sampled by the BHS. These could, for example, be cases of grave bodily injury (with lethal consequence) or qualified cases of property or sexual offenses (with lethal consequence). Further country-focused analysis is needed in order to clarify this issue, e.g., by looking into cases of grave bodily injury and property offenses, as well as sexual offenses and other potentially violent crime (with lethal consequences). Nevertheless, even after such in-depth analyses, the question of non-lethal violence (attempted homicides) and its diffusion among non-homicidal offenses would remain unresolved. This conceptual and methodological challenge in essence presents another strong argument in favor of adopting a broader approach toward (lethal) violence research by including non-lethal violence, instead of focusing strictly on (completed) homicides. Yet, at the same time, this challenge also justifies the frequent exclusion of non-lethal violence in (completed) homicide research. If attempted homicides are excluded, then many

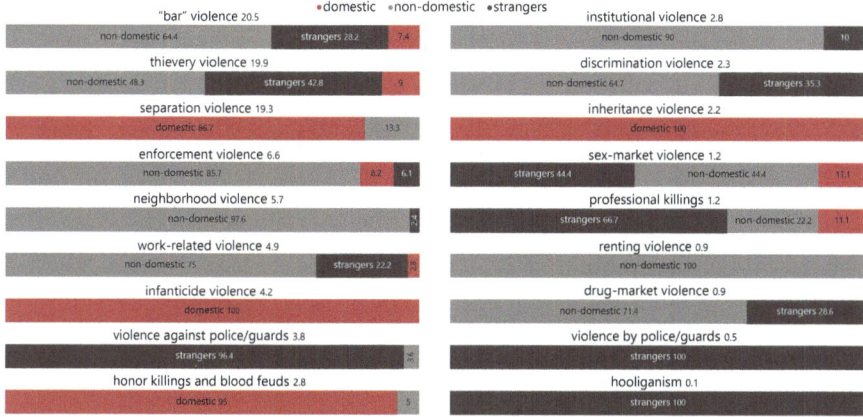

Fig. 5.3 Phenomenologically more specific types of (lethal) violence with victim-offender relationships (counting unit: case; N_{valid} 733; 1.7% missing data; in percentages)

of the above concerns become obsolete. In that sense, and from a practical and pragmatic point, the exclusion of attempted homicides and other non-lethal violence clearly makes sense and is unquestionably justified. But is it really the ideal, or at least the optimal solution for the matter at hand?

5.1.4   (Lethal) Violence Between Strangers

Homicide is mainly a convenience crime and a crime of proximity, where the offenders and the victims in most cases know each other (very) well: their interrelationships (and prior interpersonal conflicts) mainly explain the level of (lethal) physical violence, as incidents are overloaded with affect and emotion, whereas crime-related (lethal) violence between strangers is largely instrumental (Mucchielli, 2012, p. 310). Still, what about (lethal) stranger violence that is not crime related or crime-related (lethal) violence between non-strangers? Under the presumption that crime-related violence is instrumental, therefore presumably premeditated, should the victim-offender relationship even matter?

Due to the relatively small share of (lethal) thievery violence in the BHS sample (7.4% or 147 cases) on the one side, and the rather large share of non-stranger relationships within this type (57.2% or 83 cases), analyzing thievery violence among strangers (62 cases) seems unreasonable. Particularly in light of the cases stemming from six different countries and a prolonged period of time. However, it is sensible to take a closer look at the overall stranger violence in the BHS case sample and present its distribution by type of violence (Fig. 5.4). This should enable us to detect what types of (lethal) violence occur most frequently among strangers and how this differs when compared to non-stranger violence.

Although stranger violence most frequently occurs as other public violence, this type, as already mentioned, also displays a rather large share of non-stranger violence. Thievery violence seems to be a typical form of stranger violence; however, even within

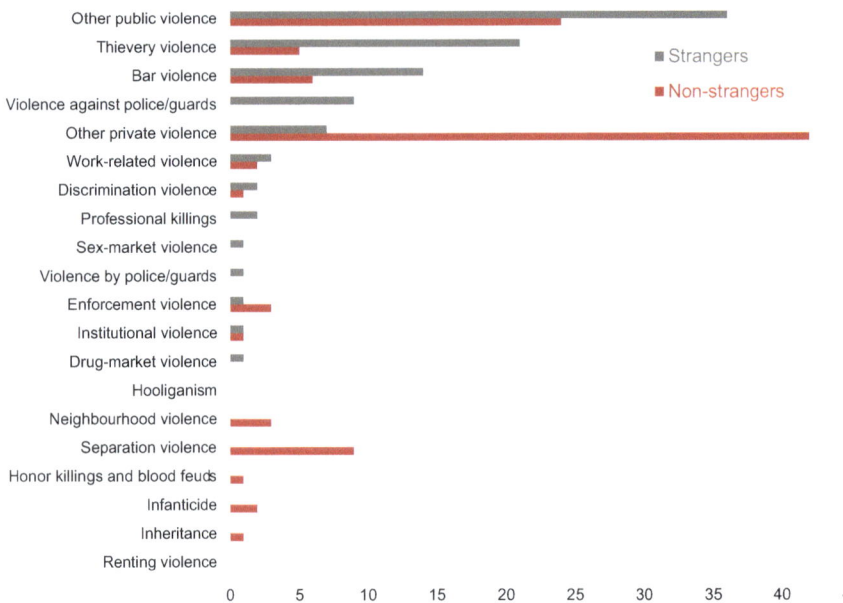

Fig. 5.4 Distribution of stranger and non-stranger victim-offender relationships by types of (lethal) violence (counting unit: case; N 1964; 1.7% missing data; in percentages)

this type, the share of non-stranger relationships between the victim and the offender is rather high. The same applies to bar violence, with an even higher share of non-stranger relationships (Fig. 5.4). Violence against or by police/guards, professional killings, as well as sex- and drug-market violence are typical forms of stranger violence. Due to classifying the cases based on the incident's situational and contextual characteristics, and in case of limited available details, the need to rely on the "privateness" or "publicness" in terms of space, we also found a significant share of stranger relationships in the other private violence category. This indicates that the (lethal) violent incident, although one between strangers, occurred in a private (non-public) setting.

In the BHS sample, we found that in only 15% of all cases (lethal), violence occurs among total strangers, whereas the majority of incidents in all countries except for Hungary involves non-domestics (friends/acquaintances). The share of (lethal) violence between domestics (including intimate partners, children, parents, siblings, and relatives) is slightly smaller. In that sense, the findings show that (lethal) violence is indeed a crime of proximity, and that in 85% of BHS cases, the offenders and the victims know each other (very) well (Table 5.2).

Focusing on Hungary and the higher share of domestic victim-offender relationships, this is likely to be connected to the higher share of female offenders in the Hungary sample (Table 5.3). Female violent offenders in the BHS and in terms of type of violence are more frequently found to have committed other *private* violence compared to males who most frequently committed other *public* violence. Likewise, female BHS offenders more frequently commit separation/divorce violence than male offenders, which then relates to the higher share of domestics in the

Table 5.2 BHS cases by country and victim-offender relationship (counting unit: case; N 1966; 1.6% missing data; in percentages)

Victim-offender relationship	BHS	HR	HU	XK	MK	RO	SI
Strangers	15.0	17.6	15.3	20.0	12.5	12.2	13.5
Non-domestics	44.3	48.0	32.3	47.7	50.0	52.8	43.6
Domestics	40.7	34.4	52.3	32.3	37.5	35.0	42.9
Cases	1966	517	606	65	88	557	133

Legend: *HR* **Croatia,** *HU* **Hungary,** *XK* **Kosovo,** *MK* **North Macedonia,** *RO* **Romania,** *SI* **Slovenia**

Table 5.3 BHS (lethal) violence offenders by gender and country (counting unit: offender) in light of population statistics (gender)

	BHS	HR	HU	XK	MK	RO	SI
% BHS offenders	100	25	32	4	5	29	6
% BHS country females	11	12	17	0	5	7	10
% Population females[a]	51.2	51.8	52.3	–	49.9	51.1	51
N_{valid}; % m.d.	2295; 1	562; 0.2	729; 0	80; 22	107; 0	671; 0.1	146; 0

Legend: *HR* **Croatia,** *HU* **Hungary,** *XK* **Kosovo,** *MK* **North Macedonia,** *RO* **Romania,** *SI* **Slovenia,** *m.d.* **missing data**
[a]Average share of females 1986–2017, source of data: World Bank staff estimates based on age/sex distributions of United Nations Population Division's World Population Prospects: 2019 Revision

Hungary sample, as this sample also displays a comparatively atypically higher share of female offenders.

5.1.5   Intimate Partner Violence

Prior research shows that stranger violence is mainly male-on-male violence, whereas intimate partner violence involves a proportionately larger share of women, especially not only as victims but also as perpetrators (Spierenburg, 2012, p. 33). Looking at the total of BHS offenders, we found that stranger violence is predominantly committed by males (96.2%) and only exceptionally by females (3.8%). Focusing on offenders' gender and the victim-offender relationships, we found that 18.8% of male offenders in our sample committed stranger violence compared to only 5.8% of females. In case of intimate partner violence, 25% of offenders are females and 75% males, while out of all offenders, 39.4% of females committed intimate partner violence compared to only 15.3% males.

Although a bit tricky, when analyzing the BHS data time-wise, we see that in those years for which the BHS sample has been assessed as most representative (2011–2014, see Fig. 4.2), the share of intimate partner violence clearly dominates over the share of stranger violence (Fig. 5.5). Thus, stranger violence seems to be

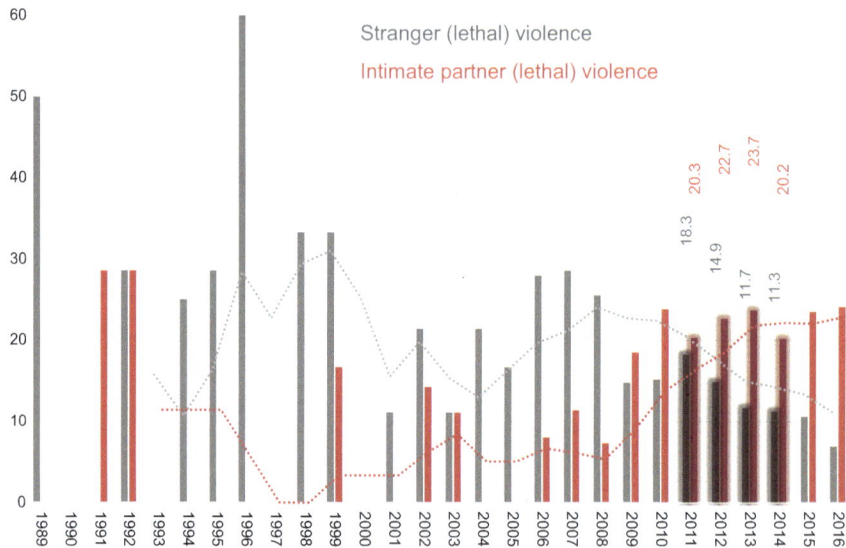

Fig. 5.5 Share of stranger and intimate partner (lethal) violence in BHS sample with 5 year moving average (counting unit: case; N_{valid} 1963; 1.7% missing data)

declining in more recent years, but such data analysis calls for cautiousness, as the aim of the BHS was not to collect data for the purpose of time series analysis, but rather to enable a first cross-sectional snapshot.

5.1.6   *(Attempted) Homicide Followed by Suicide*

Looking more closely at the specific type of (attempted and completed) homicide followed by suicide, it is clear that this is not an insignificant occurrence in the total BHS sample. Even more, if one considers that the typical homicide-suicide constellation in which the offender during or closely-timed to the violent incident commits suicide, is in fact not covered by the BHS sample. At least this is the case when it comes to completed suicides, since in such cases, there will be no prosecution against the (deceased) offender who committed suicide. In 6% of all (lethal) violence cases, the offender either commits or attempts to commit suicide (3.8% missings). While the attempted suicides might be time-related to the violent incident, the completed suicides are not. If they were, the incident could not show up in the BHS sample, since the study is based on prosecution/court files and there would be no criminal procedure launched against a deceased offender committing suicide during or closely-timed to the violent incident.

Interestingly, in Hungary (10.3%), Slovenia (9.6%), and Croatia (5.8%), (lethal) violence followed by suicides is a more frequent occurrence than in Romania (2%), North Macedonia (1%), or Kosovo (0%). Out of all (attempted) homicide-suicide cases, 78.0% of victim-offender relationships are domestic ones, 17.4%

non-domestic, and only 4.5% between total strangers. Out of these domestic relationships, 69.9% are those between intimate partners; in 17.5% of cases, the suicidal offender was the parent of the victim, while in 6.8% of cases, the suicidal offender was the child of the victim. Out of the non-domestic victim-offender relationships, 73.9% are between friends and acquaintances. Focusing on the type of violence with regard to (attempted) homicide-suicide, separation/divorce violence instantly stands out with a share of 25%, meaning that one-fourth of (attempted) homicide-suicides in the BHS is separation violence. These results are in line with findings from prior studies showing that uxoricide (the killing of an intimate partner) is the most prevalent type of violence in cases of homicide-suicide (Liem & Oberwittler, 2012, p. 200). Similarly, our findings confirm that filicide (the killing of a child) is the second most common type of homicide-suicide (Liem & Oberwittler, 2012, p. 201). One could not go so far as to say that (attempted) homicide-suicide in non-domestic (extrafamilial) relationships between friends and acquaintances in the BHS have been found to be *very rare* (17.4%), but they do constitute less than one-fifth of such cases.

The suicidal offenders are predominantly males (82.7%), when looking only at the offender-suicide variable. However, when looking at the overall distribution of offenders by gender (males 88.7% vs. females 11.3%), it becomes clear that male offenders are in fact less frequently suicidal than expected. Female offenders appear to be more suicidal (17.3%) in view of their general share in the total offender sample. This slightly higher proportion of females among the suicidal offenders cannot be explained by infanticides, since this type of violence appeared only in two cases followed by offenders' attempted suicides. This finding on extremely rare suicides when mothers commit infanticides is also in line with findings from previous studies (Liem & Oberwittler, 2012, p. 201).

Interestingly, homicide-suicide occurs more frequently in the BHS sample in case of completed (64.7%) than in the case of attempted (35.3%) homicides. Although the homicide-suicide findings originate from the offender database, the 43/57 ratio of completed vs. attempted homicides in this database corresponds quite well to the 42/58 ratio in the case database. Therefore, an approximately 70/30 ratio in favor of completed homicides in case of homicide-suicides confirms that lethal violence occurs more frequently in this type of violence. This might also indicate that homicide-suicides are indeed a distinct type of violence, as has been suggested by previous research (Liem & Oberwittler, 2012, p. 211).

Finally, looking at the *modus operandi* the suicidal offender applied, the BHS did not collect data about the suicide's *modus operandi*, but on the (lethal) incident itself and its primary victim. Here, we see that in most (attempted) homicide-suicide cases, the offenders applied stabbing (46.3%) and shooting (17.1%). Although these are also the most frequent methods applied by non-suicidal offenders (39.9% stabbing and 12.9% shooting), it seems that shooting particularly is a bit more emphasized when it comes to homicide-suicide. The role of firearms in homicide-suicide is intriguing, particularly in case of the Balkan region, where rather recent armed conflicts took place and the incidence of illegal firearm possession seems quite high. Results from prior research suggest that the availability of firearms might be one causal factor in the genesis of homicide-suicide, while firearms have also been found to be one of the main distinguishing factors between homicide-suicides and homicides only (Liem & Oberwittler, 2012, p. 212). Further research into homicide-suicides in the Balkans would be needed in order to investigate the full scope of this phenomenon, especially because the BHS did not even capture those cases where the offender committed suicide within the context of the violent incident itself.

5.1.7   Firearms and (Lethal) Violence

From the standpoint of the violent Balkan images and stereotypes (Sect. 3.1), the relevance of firearms in connection to (lethal) violence is practically self-evident. It seems plausible to assume that investigating (lethal) violence in the Balkans requires insights into the availability of small firearms and light weapons, especially in view of the tremendous influx of armaments during the "Balkan wars" of the 1990s and given that a large amount of weaponry continues to exist in the region (Grillot, 2010, p. 147). It is said that "the impact of years of civil wars in the Western Balkan region can still be felt to this day, with up to six million small arms still in circulation" (cit. German Federal Foreign Office, 2020). Notwithstanding that illegal firearms possession is a criminal offense in itself throughout all BHS countries and thus poses a challenge for national and regional security, in the context of (lethal) violence, it is necessary to check the assumption that a higher (illegal) firearms availability leads to more (lethal) violence.

At least the BHS findings do not confirm such an assumption, as merely 12.7% of all offenders in our sample used firearms, in contrast to 21.0% who used no weapon at all, or in even sharper contrast to those 62.2% of offenders who used cold weapons. Distinguishing between licensed and unlicensed (legal vs. illegal) firearms, we find that out of all offenders who used a firearm, 58% of them used an illegally possessed one and 20% a licensed one, and for 22% of offenders, the relevant data on firearm license is missing. Clearly, in case a firearm is used for committing an (attempted) homicide, the offenders in the majority of cases used a non-licensed/nonregistered one. This seems plausible considering that most of (lethal) violence incidents in the BHS were committed premeditatedly, not affectively, so that one would expect the offender to use a non-registered firearm which cannot be traced back to him/her.

Although, as stressed earlier, the BHS has not been designed for trend analyses through time, it is however worth mentioning (and thus quite indicative) that there is a noticeable decline in the share of offenders who used firearms during the 1990s and 2000s compared to the most representative time period (2010–2014). Looking at country specifics, we also see a striking difference in the share of offenders using firearms in Macedonia (38.3%), Kosovo (33.0%), Croatia (26.1%), and Slovenia (24.7%), as compared to Hungary (4.1%) and Romania (0.9%). Both these findings taken together and combined with the 12.7% of offenders using firearms in the total BHS sample, indicate that there might be a link between past armed conflicts, the availability of (illegal) firearms and their more frequent usage in violent incidents. Further analyses are obviously needed, but for the time being, it seems that in the 2010s and compared to the previous two decades, there is a decline in the incidence of firearms usage in interpersonal (lethal) violence.

One might perhaps expect, that in the case an offender used a firearm, the outcome of the violent incident is more likely to be lethal, but first descriptive analyses do not confirm such an assumption. On the contrary, in those instances when offenders used firearms, the outcome of the incident was lethal (e.g., the homicide completed) in only 48.6% of cases, whereas in cases the offender used no weapon, the outcome was lethal in 63.3% of cases. Since the completed/attempted homicide ratio in the total sample is 43/57, the inverted ratio of completed and attempted homicides in case of firearms usage does not confirm a higher lethality due to firearms usage. Now, obviously the firearms data is quite country specific and appears to be time sensitive, as well as dependent on the type of violence and affective or premeditated perpetration of the incident. Data shows that in 42.5% of incidents, the offenders acted affectively, compared to 57.5% of premeditated incidents. In the case of firearms usage, the ratio between affective and premeditated was 38/62 compared to 25/75 when no weapons were used, or 49/51 in case cold weapons were used. The lethality of the incident outcome is unquestionably determined by a combination of multiple factors, among which the usage of (illegal) firearms seems to play a less significant role, at least compared to cold weapons.

5.1.8 Alcohol and (Lethal) Violence

Prior research shows that alcohol consumption has an effect on homicide rates in Eastern Europe and that this effect varies with drinking pattern (Bye, 2008). Thus, alcohol-related homicides are more likely the result of acute arguments, more likely to be affective, and less likely to involve strangers, compared to homicides that did not involve alcohol (Spierenburg, 2012, p. 163). In view of these findings, the first issue to address relates to the potential impact of alcohol on (lethal) violence in terms of completed vs. attempted homicides. Out of all the offenders, 43.6% committed a homicide, with 56.4% attempting a homicide. Nearly 40.7% of offenders who were under the influence of alcohol *tempore criminis* completed the homicide compared to 59.3% of them who failed in their attempt to do so, while 44.2% of the non-intoxicated offenders completed the homicides compared to 55.8% who did not. There does not seem to be a markable difference between completed and attempted homicides with regard to the offenders' alcohol intoxication in the BHS.

When looking at the issue of affective (lethal) violence, out of those offenders under the influence of alcohol, 52.9% acted affectively compared to only 32.6% of affective offenders among the non-intoxicated offender group. In cases of intoxicated offenders, the victim-offender relationship is slightly less frequently one between strangers (15.1%) than in case of non-intoxicated offenders (18%). Both BHS results seem to confirm findings from previous research. Thus, alcohol seems

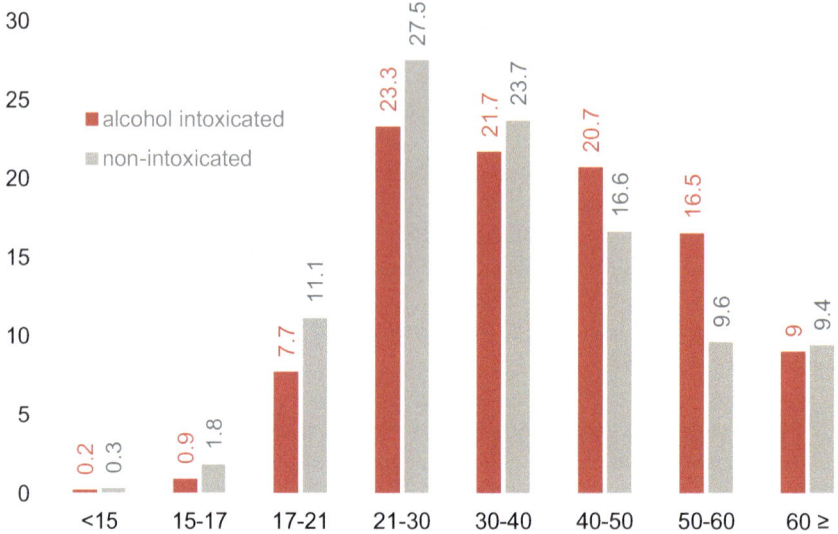

Fig. 5.6 BHS (lethal) violence offenders by age and alcohol intoxication *tempore criminis* (counting unit: offender; N$_{valid}$ 2097; 9.7% missing data; in percentages)

to have played a different role in various types of violence by victim-offender relationship: intoxicated offenders slightly more frequently engaged in violence with their intimate partners (intoxicated 19.6%, non-intoxicated 17%), siblings (intoxicated 2.9%, non-intoxicated 1.2%), friends/acquaintances (intoxicated 41.5%, non-intoxicated 35.7%), and relatives (intoxicated 7.3%, non-intoxicated 4.8%), and slightly less frequently with their children (intoxicated 2.4%, non-intoxicated 5.9%), parents (intoxicated 3.3%, non-intoxicated 6.6%), neighbors (intoxicated 3%, non-intoxicated 3.8%), and co-workers (intoxicated 2.9%, non-intoxicated 4.7%).

With regard to motive and alcohol-related (lethal) violence, there is no difference in the distribution pattern. Intoxicated as well as non-intoxicated offenders most frequently seem to be motivated by revenge (intoxicated 28%, non-intoxicated 27.3%) and greed (intoxicated 10.4%, non-intoxicated 18.1%). The most striking difference appears with respect to the category of unclear motive (intoxicated 49.3%, non-intoxicated 40.5%), which could mean that in case of intoxicated offenders, their actions were less rational and therefore more difficult to classify.

As Fig. 5.6 illustrates, alcohol-related (lethal) violence is unequally distributed among the different offender age groups, although it has a similar distribution within the overall sample in which 45.7% of offenders were intoxicated *tempore criminis*, while 54.3% were not. It seems that alcohol intoxication in the BHS plays a much more important role when it comes to lethal violence committed by offenders aged 40–50 and 50–60 than those younger than 40. This might make sense in light of the rather low share of bar violence within the BHS sample, for which commonly young males under the influence of alcohol are deemed responsible.

5.1.9 The Organized Crime Violence Nexus

It has frequently been stressed that there is a strong nexus between organized crime and (lethal) violence. Organized crime as such can be a significant source of lethal violence – it is assessed that from the start of the twenty-first century, organized crime has caused approximately the same number of killings as all armed conflicts across the world combined (UNODC, 2019, p. 12). It has thus been highlighted that organized crime is a particularly worrisome crime phenomenon in the Balkans and more broadly throughout Southeastern Europe: "The threat of organized crime is growing ever more present and powerful in the South Eastern Europe region" (cit. UNODC, 2020). And although there are plenty of evident cases of lethal violence connected to the criminal underworld throughout the region (e.g., Jovanović et al., 2020), in the whole BHS sample, only six offenders were linked to such organized crime-related violence – four of them from Hungary and two of them from Slovenia. By broadening the conception of organized crime-related violence and looking at offenders of "criminal transaction related violence," 38 such offenders were identified (1.6% of all offenders), but only 1 offender when it comes to "gang-related violence."

Out of numerous potential explanations for this rather low share of organized crime-related or illegal market-related violence, two shall be briefly addressed. First, due to methodological issues, such cases were not sampled in a representative manner. This could be a consequence of different normative frameworks or lack of prosecution of such cases (e.g., unknown offenders). It could also be that such cases are in fact in the sample, but were not identified due to deficient data collection efforts during the field work and case analysis. Although possible, this does not seem very likely. Second, there are relatively few cases of organized crime-related violence in the sampled countries, or the dark figure of such cases is very high. Due to domestic and foreign media attention on the topic of organized crime in the Balkans, such (potentially rare) incidents of (lethal) violence get picked up and reported upon extensively. This might create the impression that organized crime-related violence occurs frequently throughout the region, although compared to non-organized crime-related (lethal) violence, the incidence of such cases is extremely low (at least in the sampled countries). Most likely both explanations combined have had an influence on the BHS findings. Further research would clearly be needed in order to confirm these assumptions, but for now and based on the BHS, it seems that higher homicide rates throughout the region cannot simply be attributed to higher levels of organized crime and violence committed by or in the criminal underworld – at least not based on prosecution and court files.

5.1.10 (Lethal) Violence and Cruelty

The last topic to be discussed with regard to incident characteristics deals with (lethal) violence and particular cruelty. *Particular cruelty* was defined as an excessive amount of aggression toward the victim that can be recognized by looking at the *modus operandi* of the offender (e.g., killing the victim by burning it alive or mutilating the body of the victim). The difference in gender, age, or physical ability between the victim and the offender was explicitly disregarded, and it was made clear that with the "cruelty variable," we were not aiming to identify "normal" qualified or more severe cases, but rather looking for the "extraordinary" among the most severe cases of (lethal) violence.

In the BHS, 30 cases of particularly cruel violence were identified, all of them lethal and amounting for a total of 38 offenders. More than two-thirds of these cruel offenders acted premeditated; the majority of them were male (86.8% compared to 88.5% in case of non-cruel offenders), half of them were under the influence of alcohol *tempore criminis*, and only four were under the influence of drugs. In most instances, the offender's main motive remained unclear (20), whereas the remaining offenders acted out of revenge (11), greed (6), or (self)defense (1). The victim-offender relationship displays a different distribution pattern, with a bigger share of violence against one's children (10.5%) and intimate partners (23.7%) and a lower share of stranger violence (7.9%). Most of the "cruel offenders" were typed as having committed general private violence (24), followed by infanticide (4), separation violence (3), thievery violence (3), bar violence (2), renting violence (1), and enforcement violence (1). Clearly, particularly cruel violence is not related to public violence, at least not in the BHS sample.

Out of all the cruel incidents, the majority of cases (29) was a completed homicide, whereby 4 victims survived and 28 were killed. Cruel violence was suffered by 32 victims (28 cases with 1 victim, 2 cases with 2 victims). Not surprisingly, in almost all cases in which the offender acted particularly cruel, a psychiatric expertise was ordered (92.1% vs 67.5% non-cruel offenders). Nevertheless, "cruel offenders" were not more frequently found to be insane or of diminished criminal responsibility, both significant and insignificant (80% of cruel offenders were found fully criminal responsible vs 67.3% of non-cruel offenders). Finally, when focusing on the victims of particularly cruel violence (32), the majority of them is female (62.5%), whereby this share of female violence victims is more than twice as big as in case of non-cruel violence (28.5%), where the majority of victims is male (71.5%). This finding makes particular sense in view of the large share of domestic violence and the specific types of violence found among the cruel cases, where females commonly are far more exposed to victimization than males, as will be demonstrated in Sect. 5.3.

5.2 Offender Characteristics

After just having described the main features of (lethal) violence incidents, we now turn to the characteristics of the violent offenders. After briefly discussing the scope and potential impact of the missing data problem in the BHS offender database, key issues in merging the different databases will be addressed. This will be followed by a general overview of the findings on offender characteristics. In a next step, offender characteristics will be analyzed with respect to particular types of (lethal) violence, as well as potential risk factors such as alcohol and prior convictions for (violent) offenses. This section will provide a general overview on violent offender characteristics and potential risk factors by sample countries, as much as it will give first insight into specific offender types/groups (e.g., male violence).

5.2.1 Missing Offender Data

The BHS's offender variables (counting unit: offender; N 2321; Table 4.3) display a broader scope of the missing data problem as compared to the case variables (see Appendix). In case of the variables on BHS violence typology, victim-offender relationship, motive as well as sexual or particularly cruel *modus operandi*, this is due to having based these variables on the case descriptions (less cases than offenders). In order to analyze these (and other case-based variables) with a focus on the violent offenders, the relevant variables were included in the offender database and in case of multiple offenders duplicated accordingly. The same applies for the victim database. The methodological pitfalls of such a procedure are quite obvious. Nevertheless, this procedure appeared to be the most meaningful solution. Just as the application of the principle offence rule may somewhat distort the findings, so does this principle case rule.

More than half of the offender variables display a share of less than 5% of missing data. The most problematic variables with a share of more than 10% of missing data relate to the following: firearm license (30.8%), ethnicity (19.6%), length of prison sentence (18.7% partly due to not all offenders having been convicted or sentenced to a prison sentence), long-term prison sentence (17.9% partly due to not all offenders having been convicted or sentenced to a prison sentence), length of detention (24.4%), addiction (15.3%), legal qualifications of the offense (first instance 15.2%, final instance 14.9%, police 14.3%, prosecution 11.2%), no children and number of children (14%), drug intoxication (10.7%), and mitigated sentencing (10.3%) (see Appendix). Although far from ideal, when it comes to missing data and in view of the type of data source, the majority of variables seems suitable for analysis, while some of them need to be consumed with caution. Throughout the following paragraphs, particular cautiousness due to missing data will be indicated, wherever relevant.

5.2.2 Merging Databases with Different Counting Units

So far, throughout the analysis in this chapter, only some of the variables have been based on findings from two different databases with different counting units (case and offender as counting units). This requires a merging of the relevant databases and, as a consequence, results in either dropping or duplicating certain case data. Now, when analyzing offender characteristics in light of victim and case data, this merging of databases with dropping or duplicating relevant data becomes even more challenging and complex. Basically, a case of (non)lethal violence in the BHS commonly has one offender and one victim (81%). However, in some instances, a case has more than one offender (11%) or more than one victim (10%). Exceptionally, a case involves both several offenders and several victims (2%). In all these cases with multiple offenders and/or several victims, the merging of the three different databases (with three different counting units) requires a dropping or duplication of data. Now, when merging case data with offender or victim data (as has been done for Sect. 5.1), the duplication of relevant case data is meaningful and justified, since both offender and victim data unquestionably relate to the same case.

For example, two offenders killed three victims in a bar. When merging case data with the offender data, e.g., to find out the time of day the incident took place and whether the offenders were under the influence of alcohol or have prior convictions, then the relevant case data (time of day) becomes a new variable in the offender database, where it is duplicated for all three offenders. The same applies for merging case and victim data. In essence, such merging of data is nothing more than connecting relevant case data to the appropriate offender and/or victim in order to enable data analysis. The assumption here is that if the same variables would have been included in the questionnaire's section dealing with offender and victim data, then the values would have been the same as in the case section and identical for multiple offenders and victims within the same case. In contrast to this and when it comes to merging offender with victim data, the aforementioned assumption is simply wrong. For example, two offenders kill a man, his wife, and attempt, but fail, to kill their two children in a case of a burglary gone wrong. Simply duplicating offender data into the victim database would imply the fictional construction of two new offenders for each of the four victims. Besides "inventing" six realistically non-existent offenders and "inventing" four realistically non-existent victims in the victim or offender database (depending which one you look at), the question arises which offender and which victim should be duplicated?

Long story short – the duplication of offender and victim data in case of several offenders and/or several victims does not appear meaningful for analyzing the BHS data. Moreover, such procedure would considerably distort the findings. Therefore, the most meaningful and viable solution for the BHS is to disregard (drop) those cases that involve multiple offenders and/or victims entirely from offender-victim-case analysis. This is clearly not an ideal solution, but in light of the consequential loss of "only" 19% of all cases, respectively 23% of all offenders and respectively 22% of all victims, appears to be an optimal solution, and one that does not distorts the findings – especially if one keeps in mind that the following findings from combined offender-victim-case analysis are limited to (non)lethal violent incidents involving only one offender and one victim.

5.2.3 General Offender Characteristics

In addition to some of the more general offender characteristics that have already been discussed in relation to the incident characteristics (Sect. 5.1), such as alcohol intoxication or *modus operandi*, the following paragraphs display general findings on violent offenders' gender, age, family status, prior convictions, education and income, nationality, ethnicity, etc. Naturally, the findings need to be interpreted in light of the particular country situation, as well as the relevant (violent and non-violent) crime context. Yet, this is a task that would significantly broaden the scope and focus of this book. This will be the next big step in analyzing the BHS data in full detail and in the relevant country and crime context. The general offender characteristics will thus be displayed for the total BHS sample, as well as specific to the countries (Table 5.3).

Looking at all BHS offenders in terms of *gender* (Table 5.3) and *age* (Fig. 5.7), we see that the vast majority of violent offenders are male and only exceptionally female, whereby the group of female offenders displays an older age curve than the group of male offenders (Fig. 5.7). A similar gender distribution can be found in the different countries, whereby the share of female violent offenders is exceptionally high in Hungary, followed by Croatia, Slovenia, Romania, and North Macedonia (Table 5.3). This exceptionally high share of female offenders in the Hungarian BHS sample (17%) is clearly not a consequence of a higher share of females in the Hungarian population – the gender ratio in the BHS countries is rather constant and is approximately 1:1. The Kosovo BHS sample contains a total of 81 violent offenders, but not a single female offender, and it also displays a large share of missing data (22%). Obviously, the overall high share of female offenders in the total BHS sample is under the influence of the high share of female offenders in the Hungarian sample. Nevertheless, (non)lethal violence can clearly be characterized as a typical male type of crime in the BHS sample.

Analyzing the age curve of the offenders in the different BHS countries (Fig. 5.7, Table 5.4), for *male offenders,* we find a clear peak in the age group 21–30 (except for Hungary with a peak at 30–40), whereas the *female* age curve peaks at 30–40 or

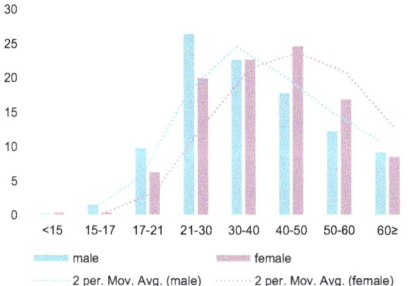 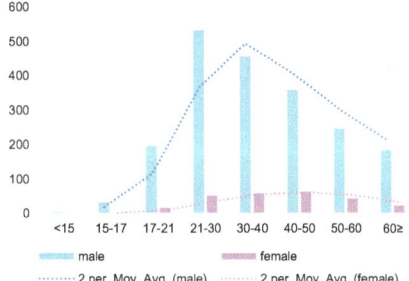

Fig. 5.7 BHS (lethal) violence offenders by gender and age groups in offender numbers (left) and as shares within gender (right) (counting unit: offenders; N_{valid} 2262; 2.5% missing data)

Table 5.4 BHS (lethal) violence offenders by age groups, gender, and country (counting unit: offender)

Age groups %	BHS ♂|♀	HR ♂|♀	HU ♂|♀	XK ♂|♀	MK ♂|♀	RO ♂|♀	SI ♂|♀
<15	0.2|0.4	0|0	0|1	0|0	0|0	1|0	0|0
15-17	2|0.4	0.8|0	2|1	0|0	0|0	3|0	0|0
17-21	10|6	6|5	11|7	16|0	11|0	12|2	3|21
21-30	27|20	25|20	22|17	33|0	33|40	29|25	32|29
30-40	23|23	20|19	26|24	16|0	24|0	23|30	21|14
40-50	18|25	20|25	18|27	24|0	14|20	15|23	22|14
50-60	12|17	15|20	13|18	5|0	9|20	11|9	10|14
60≥	9|9	13|12	9|6	6|0	8|20	7|11	12|7
N_{valid}; % m.d.	2262; 2.5	549; 2.5	714; 2.1	80; 22	104; 2.8	670; 0.3	145; 0.7

Legend: *HR* **Croatia**, *HU* **Hungary**, *XK* **Kosovo**, *MK* **North Macedonia**, *RO* **Romania**, *SI* **Slovenia**, *m.d.* **missing data**; ♂ **male**, ♀ **female**

40–50 (except for N. Macedonia and Slovenia with a peak at 21–30[2]). The male offenders are clearly younger than the female ones and it will be exciting to see whether and how this is related to the different types of (lethal) violence the offenders engage in.

There is no question that gender and age are strong predictors of criminal behavior, including violent one, just as they are, generally speaking, strong predictors of any kind of human behavior – not only criminal one. Similarly, relationship status, parenthood, education, employment and income, or prior convictions and imprisonment are commonly investigated in order to detect potential criminogenic risk factors or possible protective circumstances.[3] For a full interpretation of the BHS findings with regard to all these factors, one would need to analyze other groups of offenders (e.g., non-violent offenders) as well as general population characteristics (in each of the sampled countries). Therefore, these factors will be presented and analyzed as descriptive findings, without assessing their potential impact, which will need to be done in future country-specific analysis.

---

[2] Note: This difference in the peak of the female age curve for N. Macedonia and Slovenia is most likely due to the very small numbers of female offenders in combination with a significantly smaller sample size compared to the remaining countries.

[3] These are only those factors captured by the BHS due to their availability in the data sources (case files). Criminological research commonly also focuses on other factors that might influence (violent) criminal behavior (e.g., living conditions and neighborhood characteristics, childhood abuse, parental alcohol, and/or drug addiction), but which are not subject to the analysis at hand due to lack of relevant data in the case files.

Table 5.5 BHS (lethal) violence offenders by relationship status, gender, and country (counting unit: offender)

Relationship status %	BHS ♂|♀	HR ♂|♀	HU ♂|♀	XK ♂|♀	MK ♂|♀	RO ♂|♀	SI ♂|♀
Single	42|19	41|22	38|21	44|0	39|0	47|7	42|36
Married	29|38	34|48	18|33	56|0	53|80	29|34	22|29
Cohabitation	16|25	9|14	27|27	0|0	1|20	15|41	27|1
Divorced	10|12	11|9	15|12	0|0	5|0	6|11	7|29
Widowed	2|5	4|3	2|6	0|0	1|0	2|7	2|0
Other	1|1	2|3	1|1	0|0	2|0	1|0	0|0
N_{valid}; % m.d.	2234; 3.7	539; 4.3	703; 3.6	78; 24	106; 1	666; 1	142; 3

Legend: *HR* **Croatia,** *HU* **Hungary,** *XK* **Kosovo,** *MK* **North Macedonia,** *RO* **Romania,** *SI* **Slovenia,** *m.d.* **missing data,** ♂ **male,** ♀ **female**

Looking at offenders' *relationship status,* we observe a quite similar share of offenders who are single and those who are in a relationship if not distinguishing between male and female offenders. Most of the offenders who are in a relationship are married and less frequently live in an extra-marital relationship (cohabitation), while the single offenders are most frequently single and less frequently divorced or widowed. However, when analyzing offenders' relationship status and accounting for gender differences, we observe that male offenders are far more frequently single than female offenders, who are usually married or live in a cohabitation (Table 5.5), which is probably connected to the different age curve of male and female offenders (Fig. 5.7). Nevertheless, when combining the categories married and cohabitation, then this broader category is clearly the most frequent relationship status for both male and female offenders in the overall BHS sample, but also in the country samples, except for male offenders in Romania (mainly single) and female offenders in Slovenia (mainly single). The missing data issue is again problematic when it comes to the BHS Kosovo sample (24%), but quite modest in the rest of the country samples.

In terms of *parenthood,* most male and female offenders do have children, whereas slightly less offenders do not have any children (Table 5.6). We observe that the share of female offenders with children is far bigger than that of male offenders with children. This is probably again connected to the "older" age curve of female offenders and their more frequent marital and/or cohabitational relationship status. We also observe that this more in-depth biographical information about the offenders' family status displays far more missing data than the prior offender characteristics (Table 5.6). This is to be attributed to the lack of relevant biographical information in the analyzed case files rather than poor data collection efforts in most of the countries – the exception is again the Kosovo sample, where a high share of missing data is a rather constant feature for many of the variables (see Appendix).

Table 5.6 BHS (lethal) violence offenders by parenthood, gender, and country (counting unit: offender)

Parenthood %	BHS ♂|♀	HR ♂|♀	HU ♂|♀	XK ♂|♀	MK ♂|♀	RO ♂|♀	SI ♂|♀
Yes	54|73	53|79	52|64	51|0	74|100	54|90	56|67
No	46|27	47|21	48|36	49|0	26|0	46|10	44|33
N$_{valid}$; % m.d.	1965; 14	532; 6	669; 8	72; 30	81; 24	495; 26	146; 0

Legend: *HR* **Croatia,** *HU* **Hungary,** *XK* **Kosovo,** *MK* **North Macedonia,** *RO* **Romania,** *SI* **Slovenia,** *m.d.* **missing data,** ♂ **male,** ♀ **female**

Looking at all BHS offenders' *educational background, employment, and income,* we find that most offenders have a secondary education (high school), are mainly unemployed, and have a below-average income (Table 5.7). For most variables in the majority of BHS countries (except for Kosovo), the share of missing data is rather modest. Despite country differences, it is safe to conclude that BHS offenders have a mid- and lower-level educational background, with a noticeable share of those with no formal education at all, which applies for both genders. The category of other education includes faculty and PhD-level education, whereas the category of higher education includes an in-between-level education that follows secondary education (high school), but in contrast to a university degree faculty education, it is more practice/work oriented and typically lasts 2–3 years.

Now, the variable capturing the offenders' employment status shows that most offenders are unemployed, at least according to information contained in the analyzed case files. It is however quite common throughout the region and in the private business sector that workers are not officially registered as employees or that goods and services are offered outside the framework of a registered business. Unregistered labor markets and shadow economies throughout the region are clearly an issue to keep in mind (Botrić, 2011, p. 95). Same cautiousness is in place when contextualizing BHS findings on offenders' income, since even in cases when the workers or businesses are registered, there is a quite common practice in most of the countries to report only minimum wages or turnovers. This might very well explain the discrepancy found in the relevant BHS data, where the "no-income" data does not overlap with the "not-employed" data. This shows that some offenders, despite being unemployed, do have an income. This could however also be due to an income based on unemployment or other social grants. In any event, violent offenders in the BHS sample can clearly be characterized as a below-average or no-income group, which again goes for both genders and applies to all the BHS countries.

Criminologically speaking, *recidivism* is always a fascinating topic, particularly in relation to *new* criminal behavior and the question whether *prior* criminal behavior, captured by convictions and/or prison experience, might have played a role in the offender's criminogenesis. Obviously, the fact that an offender has no prior conviction(s) does not mean that he/she has not already committed a criminal

Table 5.7 BHS (lethal) violence offenders by education, employment, income, gender, and country (counting unit: offender)

		BHS ♂|♀	HR ♂|♀	HU ♂|♀	XK ♂|♀	MK ♂|♀	RO ♂|♀	SI ♂|♀
Education %	Secondary	45|45	57|57	41|40	24|0	40|60	43|44	44|29
	Elementary	35|35	34|25	48|47	15|0	44|0	25|15	36|50
	Higher	10|6	2|5	0.2|1	58|0	4|0	23|28	4|0
	None	7|7	2|5	10|7	0|0	10|20	7|8	15|14
	Other	3|7	5|9	1|5	3|0	2|20	2|5	1|7
	N~valid~; % m.d.	2108; 9	532; 6	653; 10	71; 31	99; 8	616; 8	137; 6
Work %	No	55|59	51|62	43|57	30|0	59|60	69|57	59|72
	Yes	33|27	28|21	46|30	69|0	31|20	24|29	26|14
	Retired	12|14	21|17	11|13	1|0	10|20	7|14	15|14
	N~valid~; % m.d.	2190; 6	536; 5	683; 6	70; 32	98; 8	662; 2	141; 3
Income %	Below average	45|52	50|52	58|62	49|0	11|25	32|30	51|29
	No income	38|33	34|38	18|20	5|0	60|50	59|53	45|64
	Average	15|14	13|10	21|17	46|0	25|25	9|15	2|7
	Above average	2|1	3|0	3|1	0|0	4|0	0|3	2|0
	N~valid~; % m.d.	2124; 9	509; 10	676; 7	73; 29	87; 19	639; 5	140; 4

Legend: *HR* **Croatia,** *HU* **Hungary,** *XK* **Kosovo,** *MK* **North Macedonia,** *RO* **Romania,** *SI* **Slovenia,** *m.d.* **missing data,** ♂ **male,** ♀ **female**

offense. The lack of prior convictions simply means that he/she has not already been *convicted* of a crime, whereas the question of whether he/she has in fact previously *committed* a crime remains unanswered. In that sense the group of offenders with no prior convictions and/or prison experiences is far less informative (due to the many unknowns of the dark figure) than the group of offenders that has been convicted and/or spent time in prison. Prior convictions were in the BHS captured as *general and specific recidivism*, distinguishing between any criminal convictions and those due to having committed a violent criminal offense. The BHS also collected data on the offenders' *prior imprisonment* and the length of the time spent in prison.

As the relevant data shows (Table 5.8), out of all BHS offenders, more than one out of three has been convicted for a criminal offense prior to the (lethal) violence incident (general recidivism: 37.7%), whereas almost one out of four has been convicted for a prior violent offense (specific recidivism: 23.7%). For 40% of male offenders, general recidivism was found and for 26% special recidivism. Only for 20% of female violent offenders general and for 9% of them special recidivism was indicated in the case files. Only 5% of female BHS offenders served a prison sentence prior to the violent incident, whereas even 23% of the male BHS offenders had already spent time in prison. Now, from a preventive perspective, it would surely be interesting to investigate whether and how offenders with an already

Table 5.8 BHS (lethal) violence offenders by type of recidivism, prior imprisonment, gender, and country (counting unit: offender)

%	BHS ♂|♀	HR ♂|♀	HU ♂|♀	XK ♂|♀	MK ♂|♀	RO ♂|♀	SI ♂|♀
General recidivism	40|20	36|18	55|25	11|0	38|0	34|14	41|7
N_{valid}; % m.d.	2202; 5	530; 6	685; 6	71; 31	105; 2	668; 1	143; 2
Specific recidivism	26|9	23|10	34|11	3|0	23|0	20|2	34|7
N_{valid}; % m.d.	2137; 8	524; 7	681; 7	64; 38	101; 6	624; 7	143; 2
None	77|95	78|92	72|94	96|0	74|100	80|98	75|100
<1 year	6|2	9|5	4|1	0|0	12|0	3|0	8|0
1-3 years	6|1	5|0	8|3	0|0	6|0	5|0	6|0
3-5 years	4|1	4|0	4|1	3|0	2|0	4|2	1|0
≥5 years	8|2	3|3	13|2	2|0	6|0	8|0	10|0
N_{valid}; % m.d.	2134; 8	520; 8	681; 7	66; 36	100; 7	624; 7	143; 2

(Column "Prison %" label appears vertically alongside the None / <1 year / 1-3 years / 3-5 years / ≥5 years rows.)

Legend: *HR* **Croatia,** *HU* **Hungary,** *XK* **Kosovo,** *MK* **North Macedonia,** *RO* **Romania,** *SI* **Slovenia,** *m.d.* **missing data,** ♂ **male,** ♀ **female**

documented violent criminal history could be approached as a high-risk target group. The missing data problem is again most pronounced in case of the Kosovo sample, but again quite modest for all the other countries.

Among the factors commonly identified to be playing a major role in violent incidents, *alcohol intoxication tempore criminis* on the side of the offender might very well be the most prominent one. This is well reflected by the BHS findings in the Croatian, Hungarian, and Romanian samples, but strangely not as pronounced in the Slovenian sample, and appears almost irrelevant in the samples from Kosovo and North Macedonia, whereby the share of missing data cannot account for this country-specific difference (Table 5.9). We observe that male offenders are more frequently under the influence of alcohol during the (lethal) violent incident than female offenders. The BHS also collected data about offenders being under the influence of drugs *tempore criminis*, but with 5.3% of such offenders, this was found to be the exception (N_{valid} 2073; missings 10.7%), especially when compared to the detected high share of alcohol intoxication (N_{valid} 2104;[4] missings 9.3%).

In those 18.2% of instances where offenders were found to have an *addiction* (N_{valid} 1966; missing data 15.3%), the vast majority of offenders suffered from an

---

[4] The discrepancy between the N_{valid} provided in the text (2104) and in Table 5.9 (2102) is the result of missing data on offenders' gender. This missing data problem regarding offenders' gender is most pronounced (again) in the Kosovo sample ($N_{missing}$ 23), but few cases are found in the Croatian ($N_{missing}$ 2) and Romanian samples ($N_{missing}$ 1) as well. These missings however relate only to the cases involving one offender and one victim – for missing data on victims' gender in the total sample, see Table 5.11 and Appendix. The short case descriptions were not always fully conclusive in this respect, so out of consistency none of the missing gender values were corrected.

Table 5.9 BHS (lethal) violence offenders by alcohol intoxication, gender, and country (counting unit: offender)

Alcohol %	BHS ♂|♀	HR ♂|♀	HU ♂|♀	XK ♂|♀	MK ♂|♀	RO ♂|♀	SI ♂|♀
Yes	47|36	53|41	50|34	9|0	9|0	53|49	33|13
No	53|64	47|59	50|66	91|0	91|100	47|51	67|87
N_{valid}; % m.d.	2102; 9	440; 22	693; 5	65; 37	101; 6	659; 2	144; 1

Legend: *HR* **Croatia,** *HU* **Hungary,** *XK* **Kosovo,** *MK* **North Macedonia,** *RO* **Romania,** *SI* **Slovenia,** *m.d.* **missing data,** ♂ **male,** ♀ **female**

alcohol addiction (83.2%), followed by multiple substance addiction (8.8%), hard drug addiction (5%), and soft drug addiction (3%).

The vast majority of offenders were citizens of the country where the (lethal) violence incident took place. This overlap in *offender citizenship* and country amounts to 100% in Kosovo, 99.1% in North Macedonia, 95.7% in Hungary, 95.4% in Croatia, and 91.8% in Slovenia (N_{valid} 2263; missing data 2.5%). The remaining offender citizenships relate to relevant neighboring countries and largely reflect other citizenships as would be expected in the general population (e.g., Serbian and Bosnian in Croatia, Romanian in Hungary, Albanian in North Macedonia, Hungarian in Romania, Bosnian and Croatian in Slovenia). Foreign citizens obviously do not constitute a noticeable share of violent offenders in the BHS sample. However, citizenship captures only the formal belonging to a country in terms of citizenship, but not one's ethnicity.

Ethnicity is far more relevant throughout the region than an actual foreigner status in terms of foreign citizenship. Therefore, the BHS also collected information on offenders' ethnicity. Compared to the rest of Europe, where migrations and foreign citizens are frequently discussed in view of their role and share in crime, migration and foreigners play a far less prominent role in Southeastern Europe. As with citizenship, there is a significant overlap between the country of incident and the offenders' ethnicity in Kosovo (97.4%), Hungary (88.7%), Croatia (85.2%), and Romania (81.9%), but not in Slovenia (67.8%) and North Macedonia (51.4%). Nevertheless, the remaining ethnicities in these two countries, just like in those with a more obvious overlap, well reflect ethnic minorities that are found in the general population. It is however interesting that in Slovenia (11%), Hungary (7.7%), Romania (7.1%), and North Macedonia (4.7%), Roma and Sinti account for a quite significant share of ethnic minorities among violent offenders (N_{valid} 1865; missing data 19.6%).

5.2.4   Male (Lethal) Violence

In light of the just presented offender characteristics and bearing in mind all the discussed main incident features (Sect. 5.1), it is challenging to pick only one further topic for analysis. Since the number and share of female offenders in the BHS sample are rather small (Table 5.10), the following paragraphs will focus on male (lethal) violence. Not only do male offenders constitute the vast majority of offenders in the BHS sample, but also their particular distribution according to the type of violence and victim's gender seems to be of great importance for understanding the phenomenology of (the most frequent) violence in the Balkans.

Most BHS offenders are male and most BHS offenders engage in (lethal) violence against male victims (Table 5.10). As explained in the section's introductory methodological part, the data for this kind of analysis deals with 81% of the BHS offender sample (N 1617). All cases involving more than one offender and/or more than one victim were dropped in order to avoid duplication/invention of non-existent offenders and/or victims. Male-on-male (lethal) violence is most expressed in the Romanian sample (the Kosovo sample displays considerably more missing data and thus only male offenders in a rather small sample), whereas male-on-female (lethal) violence is most frequent in the Hungarian sample (Table 5.10). The Hungary BHS sample also has an atypically high share of female offenders concerning both female-on-female and female-on-male (lethal) violence. There appears to be some sort of connection between the large share of female violent offenders and the large share of female victims. Further country-specific analysis should be able to detect its potential causes and provide explanations.

Analyzing (lethal) violence by offenders' and victims' gender and the type of violence (N_{valid} 1605; missing data 0.7%), we find that in the BHS sample, *male-on-male (lethal) violence* presents itself mainly as other public (36.5%) and other private violence (29.5%), followed by bar (11.8%) and thievery (4.5%) violence. The remaining male-on-male (lethal) violence displays as work-related (2.7%), neighborhood (2.6%), enforcement (2.6%), institutional (1.8%), and separation violence

Table 5.10 BHS (lethal) violence offenders and victims by gender and country (counting unit: offender)

offender | victim by gender %	BHS	HR	HU	XK	MK	RO	SI
male violence ♂|♂	63	70	45	80	73	71	64
♂|♀	25	19	37	20	20	21	25
female violence ♀|♀	3	3	7	0	1	1	3
♀|♂	9	9	11	0	5	7	8
N_{valid}; % m.d.	1607; 1	420; 1	479; 0	40; 11	74; 1	487; 0	107; 0

Legend: *HR* **Croatia,** *HU* **Hungary,** *XK* **Kosovo,** *MK* **North Macedonia,** *RO* **Romania,** *SI* **Slovenia,** *m.d.* **missing data,** ♂ **male,** ♀ **female**

(1.7%), honor killings/blood feuds (1.3%), discrimination violence (1.2%), violence against police/guards (1.1%), inheritance violence (0.9%), renting (0.6%) or drug-related violence (0.5%), with the other types accounting for less than 0.5%. In sharp contrast to this male-on-male type distribution, *male-on-female violence* mainly presents itself as other private (55.5%) and separation (22.7%) violence. This large share of other private (lethal) violence committed by male offenders toward female victims that is immediately followed by separation violence is very likely to indicate that in cases of private male-on-female violence we might actually be looking at domestic violence, potentially even intimate partner violence. Due to lack of more specific information on domestic disputes and/or separation conflicts in the short case descriptions, some of these cases very well might have been captured within the more general category of other private violence. The remaining types of male-on-female (lethal) violence are thievery (8.3%) and other public (8.1%) violence, with neighborhood (1.5%), sex-market (1.2%), enforcement (0.7%), work-related (0.7%), and bar (0.5%) violence making up for approximately 5%. The remaining types account for less than 0.5% each.

In contrast to the previously presented typology distribution of male (lethal) violence, female (lethal) violence presents itself mainly as other private violence (33.3%), infanticides (25.9%), thievery (14.8%), other public (4.3%) and enforcement (3.7%) violence in case of *female-on-female violence*. However, *female-on-male (lethal) violence* predominantly displays as other private violence (67.6%), infanticides (10.1%), separation (8.6%) and other public (4.3%) violence, followed by bar (2.2%) and thievery (2.2%) violence. Interestingly, both male-on-female and female-on-male (lethal) violence in our sample presents itself in more than 75% of cases as other private and separation violence (male-on-female 78.2%; female-on-male 76.2%). This finding shows that both male and female offenders, when acting out violently toward the opposite gender, do this commonly in a private and/or intimate context. This might then indicate that, when it comes to domestic and/or intimate partner violence, both genders display a comparable propensity toward aggressive behavior, with the difference obviously being that males do this more frequently than females.

5.3   Victim Characteristics

After just having analyzed the main offender characteristics (Sect. 5.2), we now turn to the victims of (lethal) violence. This section will first briefly discuss the missing data issue which, when it comes to the victims of (lethal) violence in the BHS and compared to the other counting units, is much more pronounced (see Appendix). The challenges of merging the different databases with the victim database are in principle the same as when it comes to the offender database and same goes for the applied solutions to this challenge (Sect. 5.2). After these methodological introductions to the victim data, the section continues by providing first findings on main victim characteristics. This will be supplemented by analyzing potential risk factors for (lethal) victimization, especially victims' alcohol intoxication.

5.3.1 Missing Victim Data

The victim variables (counting unit: victim N 2299) display a much wider range of the missing data problem as compared to the case and offender variables (Table 5.11 and Appendix), whereas the relationship databases (offender-offender relationship, victim-victim relationship, victim-offender relationship) were not analyzed at all due to the large share of missing data. The victim-offender relationship database was however used as a source of additional information in supplementing the short case descriptions if and when needed. Although quite tragic in terms of empirical research, the scope of missing data on different victim variables is nevertheless very insightful. It vividly depicts the lack of focus of criminal justice actors on the victims of (lethal) violence, at least if one agrees that the quantity and quality of information about victims (not) contained in case files might serve as a solid proxy for the (lack of) focus on the victims.

Clearly, the analyzed case files display a significant lack of information on victims' background such as education, parenthood, income, employment, addictions, and relationship status (Table 5.11). One might suspect that the lack of such data could also be due to poor data collection efforts during field work. However, this seems highly unlikely, especially when comparing the scope of missing data in the case and offender databases. To be more specific, suboptimal data collection during field work would be displayed as a constant feature throughout all databases (not only in the victim database) in the form of high missing values in most of the variables. This is however not the case with the other BHS databases in all of the sampled countries (exception: Kosovo sample). Due to the scope of missing data in the victim database, the following analysis will focus on those variables that display a less dramatic share of missing data.

Table 5.11 BHS (lethal) violence victim variables – share of missing data (counting unit: victim; N 2299)

Variables	% m.d.	Variables	% m.d.	Variables	% m.d.
Education	55.4	Affective	14.3	Injury severity	3.0
Parenthood	44.3	Alcohol	13.1	Time of death	2.8
Income	38.1	Age	10.3	Gender	2.1
Employment	31.2	Nationality	9.5	VO relationship	1.9
Addiction	29.2	Cruelty	5.9	Type	0.1
Relationship	28.6	Sexual	5.4	Motive	0.0
Ethnicity	26.1	Residence	5.3		
Drugs	15.4	Public official	4.2		

Legend: *m.d.* missing data

5.3.2 General Victim Characteristics

BHS victims of (lethal) violence in terms of gender are predominantly male and account for 88.7% of all BHS victims, and the two largest age groups of male victims are 30–40 and 20–30 years compared to the two largest age groups of female victims who are 40–50 and 30–40 years (Fig. 5.8). Comparable to the female offenders' age curve (Fig. 5.7), we again observe a slightly older age curve for female victims than for male victims (Fig. 5.8). A similar age curve in view of gender differences is found in the sample countries, again with the exception of Hungary, where just like in case of the female offenders, we find a significantly higher share of female victims (43.5%) than in all the other BHS countries, where the share of female victims ranges from 16.7% to 29.7% (Table 5.12).

In terms of particularly vulnerable groups of victims, it appears that especially older women aged 70 years and more make up a considerable share of victims of (lethal) violence. Interestingly, in the BHS sample, infants and young children appear far less exposed to (lethal) violence than the elderly. This might reflect a generally rather old population in the BHS countries with low birth rates, but further national research would be needed in order to make firm statements.

Most victims (84.3%; N_{valid} 2177) just like most offenders (80.4%; N_{valid} 2234) come from the same place where the offence was committed, which also means that in most cases, the victim and the offender come from the same place. Only exceptionally is the victim a public official targeted by the violent incident in relation to his/her duty. Looking at the severity of the injuries inflicted upon the victims in the course of the violent incident, we observe that more than 3/4 of victims suffered heavy bodily injuries (42.7%) or death (34.8%), compared to only less than one-fourth of victims who suffered light bodily injuries (16.5%) or no injuries at all (6.1%) (N_{valid} 2229). These findings show that at least on this overall level, the severity of the victims' injuries is no proxy for (potential) lethality of the violent incident, since the overall ratio of completed vs. attempted homicides among victims is 39.7 vs 57.4 (N_{valid} 2234). In other words, if attempted homicides were to be regarded as instances of less severe violence inflicted upon the victim, then the share of light

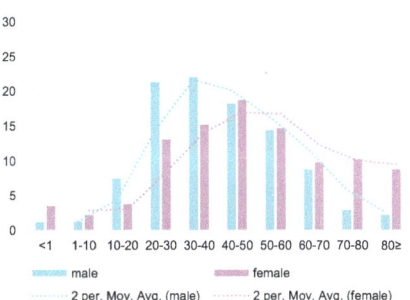 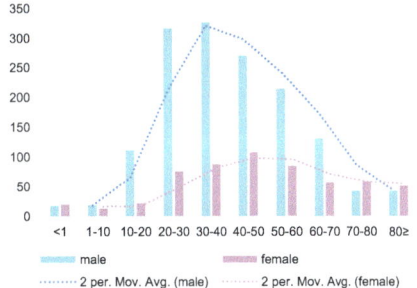

Fig. 5.8 BHS (lethal) violence victims by gender and age groups in victim numbers (left) and as shares within gender (right) (counting unit: victims; N_{valid} 2059; 10.4% missing data)

Table 5.12 BHS (lethal) violence victims by age groups, gender, and country (counting unit: victim)

Age groups %	BHS ♂|♀	HR ♂|♀	HU ♂|♀	XK ♂|♀	MK ♂|♀	RO ♂|♀	SI ♂|♀
<1	1|4	2|6	2|4	0|0	1|4	1|2	0|0
1-10	1|2	0.4|2	4|3	0|0	1|0	0.4|1	2|4
10-20	8|4	5|1	9|6	18|0	6|7	8|3	8|0
20-30	21|13	23|13	10|11	32|22	33|7	26|16	18|16
30-40	22|15	25|17	16|12	14|44	22|15	23|17	30|16
40-50	18|19	20|17	18|18	22|11	13|26	17|19	18|24
50-60	14|15	12|17	21|15	12|11	17|4	12|15	14|13
60-70	9|10	8|6	13|9	0|11	6|19	9|12	9|13
70-80	3|10	4|9	4|12	2|0	0|15	3|9	0|7
80≥	2|9	2|11	4|10	0|0	1|4	2|7	2|7
N_{valid}; %m.d.	2059; 10	576; 5	583; 17	58; 39	106; 25	589; 1	147;5

Legend: *HR* **Croatia,** *HU* **Hungary,** *XK* **Kosovo,** *MK* **North Macedonia,** *RO* **Romania,** *SI* **Slovenia,** *m.d.* **missing data,** ♂ **male,** ♀ **female**

and no bodily injuries suffered by the victims (22.6%) should be much closer to 60% (approx. share of attempted homicides) or at least far more pronounced. Similarly, when looking at the time of death of the victims in the BHS sample, we observe that a rather large share of killed victims did not die on the spot and during the violent incident itself, but later on (29%; N_{valid} 2234). Based on both findings, it (again) seems plausible to study completed as well as attempted homicides more comprehensively as one phenomenon, ideally by also including other types of non-homicidal (lethal) violent crime (e.g., aggravated assault or rape with and without fatal outcome).

Slightly more victims of (lethal) violence in the BHS sample are in a relationship (52.8%) than those who are single (45.7%), with the majority of those that are in a relationship being married (N_{valid} 1641). However, since the share of missing data for this variable (28.6%), just as for other similar victims' background variables, is rather high (Table 5.11, Appendix), it does not seem justified to base further analysis on these findings. Therefore, the last topic in the victim characteristics section will focus on the influence of alcohol intoxication *tempore criminis* in an attempt to check for potential risk factors.

5.3.3 Victimization and Victim-Offender Alcohol Intoxication

Unsurprisingly, when looking at victims' alcohol intoxication by the type of (lethal) violence, we find the highest share of intoxicated victims within bar violence, where 69% of victims were under the influence of alcohol *tempore criminis*. Now, differentiating between lethal and non-lethal violence in light of victims' alcohol intoxication, we see that in the total BHS sample, male victims are slightly more often under the influence of alcohol in case of completed homicides, and male victims are generally far more often under the influence of alcohol than female victims (Table 5.13). On the different country levels, there also seems to be a slightly higher share of intoxicated victims (especially male ones) among those who died due to the violent incident (Table 5.13). Based on first analysis and without further information, one can only speculate about the existence of actual correlations, let alone causal relations. Whether victims' alcohol intoxication is in fact a potential risk factor in view of the deadliness of the incident or not would need to be firmly established before one can further investigate how this risk factor might be working. Could it be that intoxicated victims are more helpless and less able to defend themselves in the event of a violent incident, or might it be that intoxicated victims are more likely to get involved, perhaps even provoke, a potentially deadlier violent incident? How could these questions even be empirically investigated and further explored?

Clearly, the impact of victims' alcohol intoxication *tempore criminis* cannot be analyzed, let alone understood correctly, outside of the context of the whole violent incident, which obviously includes the offender. Analyzing the potential impact of alcohol on the deadliness of the violent incident, we checked for differences between completed and attempted homicides depending on victim and/or offender intoxication (Table 5.14). We also analyzed alcohol intoxication in view of the gender variable for the most frequent victim-offender constellation (male-on-male) while distinguishing between lethal and non-lethal violence and for all the BHS countries (Table 5.15).

Table 5.13 BHS (lethal) violence victims by alcohol intoxication, gender, country, and (completed) homicide (counting unit: victim)

Alcohol intoxication %		BHS ♂|♀	HR ♂|♀	HU ♂|♀	XK ♂|♀	MK ♂|♀	RO ♂|♀	SI ♂|♀
Completed	Yes	46|15	46|13	49|15	17|0	13|10	65|23	10|8
	No	54|85	54|87	51|85	83|100	87|90	35|77	90|92
Attempted	Yes	37|12	43|14	42|13	0|0	0|0	39|12	30|10
	No	63|88	57|86	58|87	100|100	100|100	61|88	70|90
N_{valid}; % m.d.		1994; 11	413; 32	692; 2	65; 8	80; 33	591; 1	153; 1

Legend: *HR* **Croatia**, *HU* **Hungary**, *XK* **Kosovo**, *MK* **North Macedonia**, *RO* **Romania**, *SI* **Slovenia**, *m.d.* **missing data**, ♂ **male**, ♀ **female**

Table 5.14 BHS (lethal) violence victims and offenders by alcohol intoxication and (completed) homicide (counting unit: victim/offender; N_{valid} 1389; missing data 14.1%)

Homicide %	Victim and offender intoxicated	Neither victim nor offender intoxicated	Only offender intoxicated	Only victim intoxicated
Completed	33.4	45.4	14.2	7.1
Attempted	31.3	42.3	20.9	5.5

Table 5.15 BHS victims of male-on-male (attempted) homicide by alcohol intoxication and country (counting unit: victim)

Homicide %	BHS Y|N	HR Y|N	HU Y|N	XK Y|N	MK Y|N	RO Y|N	SI Y|N
Completed	57|43	54|46	68|32	33|67	17|83	71|29	12|88
Attempted	42|58	50|50	52|48	0|100	0|100	40|60	32|68
N_{valid}; % m.d.	876; 13	194; 34	209; 2	30; 6	36; 33	341; 1	66; 3

Legend: *HR* **Croatia,** *HU* **Hungary,** *XK* **Kosovo,** *MK* **North Macedonia,** *RO* **Romania,** *SI* **Slovenia,** *Y* **alcohol intoxicated,** *N* **not alcohol intoxicated,** *m.d.* **missing data**

Findings (Table 5.14) indicate that there is no apparent difference between the constellations when both victim and offender are alcohol intoxicated as opposed to when neither of them is intoxicated, at least with regard to the share of such constellations within cases of completed and attempted homicides. However, when looking at those violent incidents where only the victim or only the offender is alcohol intoxicated, the findings show that offender intoxication is more frequently found among completed homicides, whereas victim intoxication is more frequently found among attempted homicides. BHS findings (Table 5.15) also show that there is a considerable country-specific difference when it comes to victims' alcohol intoxication in case of male-on-male (lethal) violence, both with regard to the share of (non) intoxication and (non)lethality of the incident. Looking at the total BHS sample, we see that in case of completed male-on-male homicides, almost 60% of victims were under the influence of alcohol. This ratio is almost exactly inverted in case of attempted male-on-male homicides, where almost 60% of victims were *not* under the influence of alcohol. However, looking at the country findings, we see strong variations both in share and distribution of alcohol intoxication. In light of this and considering the actual sample size that covers 81% of victims and offenders (one-on-one incidents), the findings are not fully conclusive and further analysis is obviously needed, especially in order to account for the detected country-specific variations.

5.4   Procedural Characteristics

In this section, (lethal) violence is analyzed from a procedural and normative perspective. This puts the focus on offenders of (lethal) violence and how they are handled by the criminal justice system. The criminal justice system includes the police, the prosecution, and the courts. The findings deal with various procedural characteristics of criminal prosecutions and trails and also relevant trial outcomes and sentencing decisions. The goal of this line of inquiry has been to decipher the how, perhaps even some of the why, of the normative construction of (lethal) violence. However, first findings allow only for a very general impression of the main procedural characteristics. In order to further analyze and fully understand them, in-depth country-specific analyses are needed. Nevertheless, even the first general findings seem extremely valuable, especially in view of the lack of comparable previous research in the countries of interest.

5.4.1 Missing Procedural Data

Most of the procedural data (counting unit: offender or case) displays low or modest missing data ranges (Appendix). When looking at the case-based procedural variables, we find less than 5% missing data in 13 variables and less than 10% missing data in 7 variables, and the remaining 7 variables display high missings due to the dropout of cases throughout the criminal procedure and therefore are no actual issues of missing data. A slightly higher occurrence of missing data is found in the offender-based procedural variables, where the majority of variables displays missing data between 5% and 10% (15 variables), 5 variables less than 15% missing data, and 4 variables less than 20% missing data.

5.4.2 Detection of (Lethal) Violence

Most frequently, the BHS incidents came to the attention of the police on the basis of a witness call/report (64.5%) or hospital/physician's report (13.2%). Incidents also got reported to the police by the offender (6%) or a body was found (5%), while incidents rarely got reported by the victim (1.6%) (counting unit: case; N_{valid} 1933; missing data 3.2%). The vast majority of incidents, once reported to the police, were prosecuted (93.9%) and extremely rarely dismissed by the prosecution (6.1%) (counting unit: case; N_{valid} 1952; missing data 2.3%). If, however, dismissed, then this was mainly due to lack of evidence, the offender's death, or self-defense constellations.

5.4.3 Detention and Criminal Procedure

Most BHS offenders were detained at some point during the duration of the criminal procedure which followed the (lethal) violent incident. Almost 79% of all BHS offenders were detained (counting unit: offender; N_{valid} 2227), whereby detention lasted between 1 and 2251 days (mean 425; median 308; std. deviation 390). The average length of criminal procedure, capturing the time period from the incident being reported to the police until the final adjudication in court, is 36 months in case of completed and 27 months in case of attempted homicides (Table 5.16). Interestingly, the average length of criminal procedure is usually longer in case of female offenders and in case of completed homicides in Croatia, Hungary, Kosovo,

Table 5.16 BHS procedural characteristics of (attempted) homicides by gender and country (counting unit: offender)

			BHS ♂|♀	HR ♂|♀	HU ♂|♀	XK ♂|♀	MK ♂|♀	RO ♂|♀	SI ♂|♀
Average length of procedure in months (N$_{valid}$ 2096; 10% m.d.)	C		37|30	54|36	43|29	39|0	55|9	12|29	25|40
	A		27|25	40|32	31|27	25|0	39|13	16|14	24|26
Offender pleas in % (N$_{valid}$ 2126; 7% m.d.)	C	Guilty	58|56	40|52	63|60	87|0	32|50	75|50	34|25
		Not guilty	34|38	52|40	35|37	13|0	64|50	8|31	53|75
		Silent	8|6	8|8	3|3	0|0	5|0	17|9	13|0
	A	Guilty	51|51	29|25	61|64	88|0	19|0	58|58	58|75
		Not guilty	38|40	65|69	37|31	12|0	75|100	20|19	41|25
		Silent	11|9	6|6	2|4	0|0	6|0	22|23	2|0
Convicted offenders in % (N$_{valid}$ 2152; 6% m.d.)	C		90|89	79|78	91|91	100|0	76|100	99|94	90|100
	A		90|79	79|69	91|81	95|0	83|100	98|96	81|56
Prison sentence in % (N$_{valid}$ 1915; 0% m.d.)	C		98|95	97|71	99|99	95|0	89|100	100|100	100|100
	A		98|94	96|96	100|94	97|0	94|100	98|100	98|60
Prison sentence suspended in % (N$_{valid}$ 1885; 2% m.d.)	C		3|9	8|24	2|7	0|0	0|0	2|7	2|0
	A		15|26	8|21	7|27	0|0	3|33	25|29	21|25
Harsh sentence in % (N$_{valid}$ 1859; 3% m.d.)	C		23|7	21|17	26|6	46|0	5|0	1|17	6|0
	A		2|2	1|0	5|0	0|0	0|33	1|0	2|33
Average sentence length in months (N$_{valid}$ 1859; 3% m.d.)	C		173|128	147|139	203|132	174|0	125|108	148|120	216|83
	A		63|56	39|28	105|80	25|0	74|52	56|47	50|90

Legend: *HR* **Croatia,** *HU* **Hungary,** *XK* **Kosovo,** *MK* **North Macedonia,** *RO* **Romania,** *SI* **Slovenia,** *m.d.* **missing data,** ♂ **male,** ♀ **female,** *A* **attempted homicide,** *C* **completed homicide**

and Macedonia, while criminal proceedings are much shorter in Romania and Slovenia, where in case of female offenders, proceedings are longer and the difference between attempted vs. completed homicides is less pronounced or even goes in favor of the completed homicide proceedings. It does not appear as if this average length of procedure is related directly to how the offenders plea in these countries. A considerable share of BHS offenders plead guilty, both in case of attempted and in completed homicides, and in case of both genders, with Slovenia having the lowest share of guilty pleas and Romania one of the highest.

The court proceedings commonly result in a conviction, whereas those offenders who are not convicted are rarely acquitted or charges against them dismissed. They are mainly found insane and committed to a psychiatric institution. Convictions are high for both completed and attempted homicides, whereby convictions almost exclusively result in a prison sentence (Table 5.16). Just as the prison sentence is more often suspended in case of attempted homicides, so is the issued prison sentence in case of completed homicides more often a harsh one. In this respect, a harsh prison sentence implies a long-term prison sentence. The average sentence in case of completed homicides is much longer (mean 167; median 144; std. deviation 105) than in case of attempted homicides (mean 62; median 48; std. deviation 54). Nevertheless, the still rather high sentences in case of attempted homicides indicate that these incidents are quite severe, even though they have not resulted in the death of the victim(s).

Clearly the previously provided first findings present but a fraction of the BHS procedural data which will also need to be further analyzed, both in light of specific national (normative) contexts and in light of different incident, offender, and victim characteristics. Thus far, we did not analyze the normative (re)construction of (lethal) violence by different criminal justice agencies. This means that the BHS's first line of inquiry into the "power to define violence" still remains open and is in need of further analysis (and data sourced from police files) by taking a much broader approach to (lethal) violence that also includes non-homicidal (lethal) violence.

References

Allison, P. D. (2002). *Missing data*. Thousand Oaks: Sage.

Botrić, V. (2011). Structural unemployment and its determinants in Southeast Europe. *Ekonomska Misao i Praksa, 1*, 81–100.

German Federal Foreign Office. (2020, January 31). *Working together to stop illegal arms trade in the Western Balkans*. https://www.auswaertiges-amt.de/en/aussenpolitik/themen/abruestung/uebersicht-konvalles-node/-/2118584. Accessed 2 Nov 2020.

Grillot, S. R. (2010). Guns in the Balkans: Controlling small arms and light weapons in seven Western Balkan countries. *Southeast European and Black Sea Studies, 10*(2), 147–171.

Jovanović, B., Dojčinović, S., & Đokić, S. (2020, May 5). *Bad blood: A war between Montenegrin cocaine clans engulfs the Balkans*. https://www.occrp.org/en/balkan-cocaine-wars/a-war-between-montenegrin-cocaine-clans-engulfs-the-balkans. Accessed 2 Nov 2020.

Liem, M., & Oberwittler, D. (2012). Homicide followed by suicide in Europe. In M. Liem & W. Pridemore (Eds.), *Handbook of European homicide research* (pp. 197–215). New York: Springer.

Mucchielli, L. (2012). Homicides in contemporary France. In M. Liem & W. Pridemore (Eds.), *Handbook of European homicide research* (pp. 301–312). New York: Springer.

Riedel, M., & Regoeczi, W. C. (2004). Missing data in homicide research. *Homicide Studies, 8*(3), 163–192.

Spierenburg, P. (2012). Long-term historical trends of homicide in Europe. In M. Liem & W. Pridemore (Eds.), *Handbook of European homicide research* (pp. 25–38). New York: Springer.

Stamatel, J. P. (2012). The effects of political, economic, and social changes on homicide. In M. Liem & W. Pridemore (Eds.), *Handbook of European homicide research* (pp. 155–170). New York: Springer.

UNODC. (2019). *Global study on homicide 2019, Booklet 1: Executive summary*. Vienna: UNODC.

UNODC. (2020). *UNODC South Eastern Europe on organized crime*. https://www.unodc.org/southeasterneurope/en/organized-crime/index.html. Accessed 2 Nov 2020.

Chapter 6
Key Findings and Preliminary Conclusions

Abstract Like with any research, at the end of the day, or in our case, at the end of
the book, one contemplates about "What did we find out?" This chapter explores
that question with regard to the BHS and its key findings as well as current (lethal)
violence research in more general terms. After a critical assessment of whether and
how the BHS's key findings provide answers to the research questions we put before
us, the challenge of capturing and measuring the *physics of (lethal) violence* shall be
briefly discussed. The chapter at hand thus includes a selection of the study's key
findings on the two different lines of research we had in mind when designing the
BHS: the normative construction and the empirical realities of (lethal) violence in
the Balkans. This is closely related to a few concluding remarks about the defin-
ability, measurability, severity, and "homicidality" of violence. The aim is to high-
light the underutilized potential of criminological violence research in the context
of criminology's transdisciplinary nature. The chances and limitations of future
(lethal) violence research and its prevention, at least in my opinion, first and foremost depend on our willingness and ability to fundamentally innovate the scientific
way in which we think about and look at violence.

Keywords BHS key findings · Phenomenology of violence · Physics of violence ·
Power to define violence · Homicidality · Transdisciplinary violence research

6.1 The BHS Research Questions in Light of Its Findings

Clearly, with the BHS and its first findings, as presented in this book, a considerable
gap in European homicide research has been filled, while shedding first light on the
phenomenology of (lethal) violence in this part of Europe. Although the empirical
vacuum in regionally comparable homicide research has thereby been shrunk, the
detected theoretical vacuum still needs to be addressed. The same goes for the
empirical investigation of the power to define violence. Despite the BHS having
captured the normative definition of (lethal) violence by police and its consequent
redefinition by prosecutions and courts, due to lack of data from police files,

© The Author(s) 2021

A.-M. Getoš Kalac, *Violence in the Balkans*, SpringerBriefs in Criminology,
https://doi.org/10.1007/978-3-030-74494-6_6

missing data issues and having adopted a "narrow" concept of (lethal) violence excluding non-homicidal offenses, this line of research remains largely unanswered and calls for further criminological attention.

The BHS's second line of inquiry, however, was successfully addressed and with the presented first findings provides for an original empirical glimpse into the realities of (lethal) violence in the Balkans. Slightly deviating from the initial cooperation agreements covering core countries of the Balkans,[1] the study managed to capture the phenomenology of (lethal) violence in six Southeastern European countries: Croatia, Hungary, Kosovo, North Macedonia, Romania, and Slovenia. This provides a strong basis for starting to unravel the *Balkan-violence-paradox*, while enabling critical questioning of common violent Balkan images and stereotypes.

So, in a nutshell, most of our research questions have been addressed successfully with the BHS, and many of them could already been answered. Nevertheless, many of our research questions require further country-focused and topical in-depth analysis as well as future research, while it is safe to say that in the process of conducting the study, we managed to raise more questions than answers provided. In addition to the great general scientific value of the study and its empirical findings, on a more individual note the BHS has also been a tremendous(ly exhausting) learning experience and thus an eye-opener with regard to the current criminological (un) measurability of (lethal) violence. Being interested in finding out how (lethal) violence displays itself in the Balkans, I vividly remember the disappointment I felt while skimming through the first datasets, fully realizing that overall we were not capturing, let alone measuring, the realities of violence, but rather counting some sort of its artificial (normative) construction.

If one is interested in finding out whether or why one country or region is "more violent" than another, as differences in homicide rates might imply, then it is not enough to simply look at incident, offender, or victim characteristics, let alone normative classifications, typologies, or mode of operandi. One needs to somehow capture and measure the actual violence that occurs in each incident and thereby focus on the *tangibles of violence*, not their (re)interpretation by various different actors, oneself included. In essence, one would need to capture the mere physics of violence and then come up with a purely criminological weighting and classification system of violence. Although with the BHS itself we did not even attempt to take this path, in the process of conducting the study, in fact, *due to* conducting the study and analyzing its data, this highly intriguing task emerged and is thus currently being explored by the Violence Research Lab.

---

[1] Though initially agreed with partners from Albania, Bosnia and Herzegovina, Croatia, North Macedonia, Serbia, and Turkey, the BHS could not be implemented in Albania, Bosnia and Herzegovina, and Turkey, whereas the field work has partially been conducted in Serbia, but without any indication when or if the BHS data will be made available.

6.2   The Power to (Re)Define and Deal with (Lethal) Violence

The BHS's first line of research into criminal justice actors' *power to define violence* has been discussed extensively throughout all chapters by providing numerous examples and highlighting its main conceptual, methodological, and practical research implications. Nevertheless, the empirical investigation of the "hows" and "whys" when it comes to the *normative and social construction of violence* and its (re)definition by different criminal justice actors calls for further research. In particular, by broadening data sourcing to include police files, while focusing not "only" on (attempted) homicidal violence, but by broadening the focus toward a much wider range of non-homicidal, yet clearly violent offenses (e.g., assault, robbery, rape with and without lethal consequence) and violent incidents which formally do not even constitute a criminal offense (e.g., justifiable killings).

Thus, if one aims at fully understanding the normative construction of lethal violence, then special attention should be paid to the *dark figure of homicides* as well as *homicide drop-outs*. European research has shown that a rather large share of (potential) homicides remains well hidden among natural (unsuspicious) deaths. It seems very likely that this is also the case in Southeastern Europe – at least for Croatia preliminary inquiries confirm a high likelihood for this.[2] The BHS findings show that once a homicide case, attempted as well as completed, gets investigated by the prosecution, the share of case drop-outs is extremely low. The same applies for the share of case drop-outs on the court level, whereas the share of case drop-outs on the police level remains largely unknown. Since for criminal offenses in general the share of drop-outs of reported cases is largest on the police level, it is plausible to assume that the same might apply for completed homicides and even more for attempted ones. This matter deserves further research attention and a much stronger focus on initial (lethal) violence detection, reporting, police practices, and criminal investigations.

Though our first line of inquiry into the power to define (lethal) violence focuses primarily on criminal justice actors, it is sensible to discuss the *role of researchers* at this point as well. We also have the power to define (lethal) violence and rather frequently make use of it, arguing for and against various approaches based on conceptual, methodological, and practical reasoning. With the BHS, we conceptually

---

[2] In contrast to common practices in other European countries (e.g., Germany), in Croatia coroner's inquests are not always performed by doctors of medicine but also by medical technicians. Moreover, except for Croatia's capital and few major cities, where doctors of forensic medicine usually perform the inspection of corps and issue the death certificate after having determined the probable cause of death, in most instances medical technicians decide whether an autopsy gets conducted or not. Now, this does not necessarily imply that the decisions of medical technicians about probable causes of death are less accurate than those of doctors of (forensic) medicine, or that they more frequently wrongly certify a natural (unsuspicious) death instead of a suspicious death in need of an autopsy and further investigation. It does however raise the question about the reliability of official homicide statistics and makes one wonder whether the dark figure of homicide in Croatia might not be even bigger than the one assessed for other European countries.

defined *violence as the human infliction of physical harm upon another person*, whereby the adjective "lethal" denotes that as a consequence another person has died. Such an approach is very narrow, as it focuses "only" on the undisputable core of violence: the infliction of physical harm. Yet it is at the same time also extremely broad, as it is not limited by any subjective element on the side of the offender (e.g., intent or motive) or the victim (e.g., consent or provocation), nor by various normative constructs (e.g., criminal responsibility or justifiability). Nevertheless, practically we sampled "only" lethal and non-lethal homicidal violence and discovered that with regard a rather large number of variables there appear to be no markedly differences between attempted and completed homicides. However, since we also found certain key variables which display noticeable differences when comparing attempted and completed cases, it remains unknown to what extent and how the lethality of a violent incident is related to different situational, criminogenic, or victimogenic factors and either good or bad fortune on the side of the victims.

After having sampled a total of 2073 cases involving 2416 offenders and 2379 victims of (lethal) violence, only 3.7% of sampled cases, 3.9% of offenders, and 3.4% of victims dropped out from our analysis due to lacking a violent element. This alone is a strong indication that attempted homicides are not simple cases of "nearly" or "maybe" homicidal violence, but that they might in fact be far more violent and severe than one would have initially assumed. This finding is further confirmed by the rather severe sentences imposed on attempted homicide offenders (98% prison sentence for males and 94% for females), which is in line with the type of sentence in case of completed homicides (98% prison sentence for males and 94% for females). Another indication of the severity of attempted homicide cases is the quite long average duration of the imposed prison sentences, with a mean of approximately 5 years, compared to completed homicides, with a mean of approximately 14 years. Another strong indication of the severity of attempted homicide cases which we detected with the BHS is the harmfulness of suffered violent victimization. The vast majority of BHS victims, actually more than three fourths, suffered heavily bodily injuries (42.7%) or death (34.8%), compared to only 16.5% who suffered light bodily injuries or even fewer 6.1% who suffered no injuries at all. Given that the ratio of completed vs. attempted homicides among the victims is 39.7 to 57.4 one would have expected a far larger share of victims with less severe or no injuries that comes much closer to 57.4, than does the detected share of 22.6%.

The BHS findings do not indicate that *homicides* are a unique phenomenon, something essentially different than *lethal violence* or the deadly outcome of *violence*. Based on our findings, as well as the compelling conceptual and methodological argumentation provided in the previous chapters, the exclusion of attempted homicides from homicide studies appears generally unjustified and reasonable merely due to practical research considerations and limitations. Therefore, it might be fundamentally wrong to approach the question of homicide or (lethal) violence as a dichotomy. We might rather want to approach the matter in terms of gradations or scales of a violent incident's "homicidality," as will be further discussed in the final section of this chapter (Sect. 6.4).

6.3 The Phenomenology of (Lethal) Violence in the Balkans

Now, what did we actually find out about (lethal) violence in the Balkans? The BHS data shows that there are *no major differences between attempted (58%) and completed (42%) homicides* regarding the place where the incidents occurred, their micro-locations, the time of day of the incident, the period of the week, the number of offenders and victims, (non)premeditated commission of the offense, the offenders' main motives, the general victim-offender relationship, and the offenders' alcohol intoxication *tempore criminis*. Most (lethal) violence in the BHS occurs in rural cities, closely followed by urban ones, with the least taking place in the countries' capitals that are also the biggest cities in each of the sampled countries. The majority of (lethal) violence is committed in a private micro-location in the evening (18.00–24.00) and afternoon (12.00–18.00) on the weekends and the day prior/after the weekends. The vast majority of (lethal) violence involves only one offender and only one victim. Slightly more incidents are premeditated than committed affectively, with approximately half of the offenders' motives remaining unclear, followed by revenge and greed. The victim-offender relationship is commonly one between non-strangers, whereas approximately the same share of offenders was alcohol intoxicated *tempore criminis* in case of attempted as well as completed homicides.

We did however observe *noticeable differences between attempted and completed homicides* when looking more closely at the specific victim-offender relationship and the type of (lethal) violence. Completed homicides are commonly found among domestics (between intimate partners and core family members), whereas in case of attempted homicides a non-domestic victim-offender relationship is most frequent (between friends/acquaintances and strangers). This somewhat more pronounced lethality of violence among domestics is well reflected in the most frequent types of violence in case of completed homicides, where other private violence clearly makes up for the majority of cases. Looking at attempted homicides we see that slightly more frequently the violence type is that of other public, closely followed by other private violence. Now, it might be that the lethality of a violent incident is under the impact of the incident's micro-location (private), or the victim-offender relationship (domestic). Probably it is a combination of both, as well as the impact or certain offender and victim characteristics (gender, age, specific alcohol intoxication combinations of offenders and victims, etc.), that might help explain and potentially even predict the lethality of violence. Cautiousness is however in place, since the BHS findings are under the (so far non-assessable) influence of sampling decisions (e.g., excluding assaults, robbery, and rape, with and without lethal consequences), various normative constructs (e.g., intent and negligence or justification), an unknown dark figure, and missing data – to name but a few.

As throughout Europe, (lethal) violence between complete strangers is the exception in the BHS (less than 15% of cases). Most stranger-violence can be classified as other public violence, followed by thievery and bar violence. The majority of (lethal) violence in all countries except for Hungary involves non-domestics (friends/acquaintances), whereby the findings for Hungary (more domestics) might be explained by the comparably atypically high share of female offenders (17%), for whom we in the BHS overall found to most frequently commit other private and separation/divorce (lethal) violence. Stranger-violence in the BHS is predominantly committed by males, whereas out of all offenders only 15% of males committed intimate partner violence, compared to as much as 39% of females committing intimate partner violence. Clearly, in the BHS males more often commit (lethal) violence, but in doing so mainly act out violently against males. Females however, although less frequently committing (lethal) violence, when acting out violently do so mainly against males (72% of female offenders) and in the form of other private and separation/divorce violence.

Despite the easier availability of firearms, due to the region's recent war-legacy, we found that in the BHS only 13% of offenders used firearms, compared to as much as 62% who used cold weapons and even 21% who used no weapons at all. Similarly, the organized crime violence nexus could not be confirmed by BHS findings, as even after adopting a very broad concept of organized crime related (lethal) violence, only 1.6% of all offenders could be at least vaguely linked to the criminal underworld. This is in my opinion more likely to be a consequence of unknown offenders in such cases, resulting in their no-show in the BHS sample (no prosecution against unknown persons), than an accurate reflection of the realities of (lethal) violence in the Balkans. Further systematic research, for example, analysis of media reports and expert interviews with organized crime and homicide investigators would be needed in order to confirm this assumption.

Interestingly, in particularly cruel cases of lethal violence, although extremely rare in the BHS, the offenders are less frequently found to be insane or of diminished criminal responsibility, whereas the victims are predominantly female (62.5%). This share of female victims is more than twice as big as in case of non-cruel lethal violence (28.5%), where the majority of victims is male (71.5%).

Coming back to the *Balkan-violence-paradox*, a phenomenon where we see comparably higher homicide rates throughout the region, although the Balkans do not fit a high crime profile, the BHS findings indicate that the paradox might perhaps be explained by more frequent other private and intimate partner (lethal) violence. Whether and how this should be interpreted in the context of Balkan-typical *patronage networks* remains dubious at best and needs further investigation, especially with regard to reporting and investigating cases of (lethal) intimate partner violence and possible "influences" on legal qualifications, prosecutions, charges, and convictions. Here undoubtedly all the relevant criminal justice actors (police, prosecution, and courts) have considerable latitude in their qualifications and decisions which might be under the influence of patronage networks. Put a bit more frankly, it would be highly surprising if this area of criminal justice practices, just as in case of organized crime-related (lethal) violence, should prove immune to the influence of patronage networks, while the judiciary in general, alike other public institutions, is commonly found to be highly corrupt throughout the whole region.

Now, what about the *violent Balkan images and stereotypes*? The BHS findings do not provide grounds for such stereotypes, at least not when looking at the types of (lethal) violence and the rather exceptional occurrence of honor killings or hate/discrimination violence. Even bar violence, accounting for approximately the same share as thievery violence, is a rather seldom occurrence when compared to intimate partner violence. Contemplating about the genesis and persistence of these violent Balkan images, particularly like the one presented in the example (Sect. 3.1), I wonder whether both might not be rooted in diverse cultural aspects and lacking insights into what is regionally considered customary and appropriate behavior in contrast to what is regarded as offensive and even provocative. While the refusal to have one bought a round of drinks in a bar might appear completely trivial to someone outside the region, someone who probably not even (fully) comprehends the meaning and importance of such a gesture within the broader context of a regional culture of hospitality and honor, locals will commonly perceive such a refusal as a public slap in the face and a grave insult and provocation. Consequently, someone lacking knowledge of or empathy for such regional or local cultural aspects might easily jump to the conclusion that people from the Balkans and even Southeastern Europe, who shoot at another person for refusing a drink, are "easy on the trigger" and "bloody-minded." But if one were to interpret the same violent incident by understanding the actual meaning of refusing a drink as a public slap in the face, this trigger might not appear so trivial anymore, even to someone from outside the region. Obviously the investigation and understanding of (lethal) violence, just as any other criminal and therefore also social phenomenon, must be imbedded in its cultural context in order to evade void interpretations that may lay the path for unfunded stereotypes. Similarly, and in line with what *Liem* (Chap. 2) calls for, not only (lethal) violence needs to be embedded in its cultural context, but homicide research as well. Various cultural aspects in violence/homicide research need to be discussed more frequently and much more transparently, and should probably even be far stronger accounted for, particularly if we aim at successfully joining forces in a truly European shot at homicide research.

6.4   On the Definability, Measurability, Severity, and Homicidality of Violence

Unsurprisingly, much of what we currently know about (lethal) violence, just as the findings presented in this book, depends on how and why we look at it. Some would argue that violence is any kind of (non)action causing any sort of harm to any living being. Others, myself included, would argue that violence is the human infliction of physical harm upon another person. Yet others would add to this the need for intentionality, criminal liability, or lack of justification on the side of the perpetrator and a lack of consent or provocation on the side of the victim. Thus, one might want to distinguish between violence with a lethal consequence (lethal violence) and homicides, or rather not. This is not merely a minor variation in different approaches to (lethal) violence or (attempted) homicides, but a fundamental conceptual discrepancy, a *Balkanization of concepts*, which undoubtedly also impacts violence and homicide research, as much as the knowledge it produces.

I wonder what the current state of art in property crime research would look like if we were to start off from comparably distant or Balkanized concepts of the terms "property" or "stealing"... we would probably end up at considering all types of crime as some manifestation of stealing, like stealing someone's life, sexual freedom, and personal dignity. Although legit reasoning lies behind it, such diffusion of different phenomena under the umbrella of property crime would almost certainly create more confusion and misunderstandings than actual criminological knowledge. Violence and its lethal extreme is a tangible, capturable, and measurable phenomenon that occurs in reality. As such, it can and therefore should be conceptualized and then defined based primarily on objective and empirically measurable elements. Normative constructs most certainly are not among such objective and empirically observable or measurable elements. Criminology in general would do well by developing its own "criminal vocabulary," just as (lethal) violence/homicide research might want to discuss more vigorously its fundamental concepts and definitions of violence, independently from preconceived disciplinary paradigms, practical conveniences or political agendas. The operational implementability of a purely criminological concept and definition of (lethal) violence is a consequential, but also solvable methodological issue, and therefore no excuse for the ongoing diffusion in violence research.

Besides the apparent conceptual and definitional challenges violence/homicide research is facing, there is also the challenge of measuring violence and accounting for its varying severity and harmfulness. The question is not *if* violence can be measured, but rather *how* such measuring can be achieved objectively and by relying solely on empirical facts, rather than normative constructs or pure speculations about motive, intent, or comparable subjective elements of an offense. By blending out such constructs and speculations about the subjectivities of (lethal) violence and its teleological severity we should be able to develop an *authentic criminological violence classification system*. A precondition to this is figuring out a *universal measure of violence* that should be based in and designed out of the *physics of violence* itself, not its social or normative or even disciplinary perception and (re)interpretation. Here first and foremost criminology with its inherent transdisciplinary nature is called upon to determine and weigh the physical variables of violence, such as the force needed to cause a certain injury, while accounting for the fragility of the attacked body, the duration of the attack, the force-multiplying or -mitigating effect of a used tool or weapon, the pain inflicted on the victim, and the attacked body part's vitality – to mention but a few.

Ultimately, a universal measure for violence could be used to design a scale of "homicidality" that would lead us out of the current include-exclude dichotomy in homicide research, while enabling us to look at (lethal) violence more accurately, more realistically, and much more meaningfully. Clearly, this is a task involving experts and researchers from "distant" disciplines in a setting that far surpasses what we commonly consider interdisciplinary. Working on the physics of violence and in an attempt to develop such a universal measure of violence and weight its "homicidality," in the Violence Research Lab, we spent countless hours discussing violent incidents and homicides with physicists and doctors of forensic medicine. So far we have learned that the task is extremely complex, requires transdisciplinarity, and is still often times simply too much for our own disciplinary limitations. Nevertheless, it has proven worth the effort and has already provided us with a completely new take on (lethal) violence and what violence research could and should look like, as well as what the value and implications of probable findings might be. But with this we already enter a new topic and an entirely different discussion which should be the subject of another book.

To conclude, the BHS and its first findings, as presented throughout the previous chapters, are an utmost important first step in understanding (lethal) violence in the Balkans. As such, it has clearly not solved any of the grand mysteries of homicidal violence in Southeastern Europe. However, if it has managed to raise at least some good questions, while making available original and comparative empirical data on (lethal) violence from six countries of the region, then the goal of this book has been reached.

Appendix: Scope of Missing Data by Variable and Country

BHS Case Database

Variable name	Sample name / Missing data in %						
	Croatia	Hungary	Kosovo	North Macedonia	Romania	Slovenia	BHS
proj_case_no	0	0	0	0	0	0	0
nat_case_no	0	0	0	0	0	0	0
country	0	0	0	0	0	0	0
case_terminated	0	0	0	0	0	0	0
attempt_legal_qual_3	0	0	0	0	6.5	1.5	2
completed _legal_qual_3	0	0	0	0	1.4	0	0.4
national_legal_qualifi	0.4	50.8	0	4.2	0.7	0	15.9
national_legal qualifi_new	0	0	0	4.2	0.2	0	0.3
source_city	0	0	0	0	0.2	0	0.1
pol_attention	6.2	2.8	9.6	2.1	0.9	0.8	3.2
date_report	4	0.3	6.8	1	1.9	1.5	2.1
invest_start	3.5	0.3	24.7	3.1	1.6	2.3	2.7
shorten_proced	8.1	0	52.1	1	1.4	0	4.5
case_dismiss	0	0	21.9	0	5.1	0	2.3
dismiss_date	1.5	0.3	21.9	3.1	5.4	0.8	3.1
dismiss_reason	1.9	0.2	21.9	1	5.4	0	3
indict_issued	0.4	1	17.8	4.2	0.5	2.3	1.6
indict_confirm	21.8	1.2	27.4	13.5	44.7	1.5	20.5
trial_start	1.5	1	30.1	2.1	1.8	7.5	2.9
first_adjudic	1.9	0	8.2	4.2	1.6	2.3	1.6
appeal	1.3	0	11	2.1	1.9	0	1.4
appeal_freq	1.9	0.2	34.2	4.2	2.3	0	2.7
repeat_trial	7.5	7.8	56.2	4.2	6.7	7.5	9
final_adjudic	3.3	0.2	24.7	5.2	0.2	0	2.1
witness_hearing	9.1	5.1	12.3	5.2	3.2	6.8	6
search	5.8	0	11	2.1	0.4	0	2.1

© The Author(s) 2021

A.-M. Getoš Kalac, *Violence in the Balkans*, SpringerBriefs in Criminology, https://doi.org/10.1007/978-3-030-74494-6

BHS Case Database

	Sample name	Missing data in %						
Variable name		Croatia	Hungary	Kosovo	North Macedonia	Romania	Slovenia	BHS
wiretap		6.6	0	5.5	1	0.2	0	2
autopsy		4.8	0	2.7	0	0	0	1.4
balistic_exam		8.1	0	8.2	0	0	0	2.4
drug_analysis		8.3	0	6.8	0	0.9	0.8	2.7
other_eviden		6.6	0	19.2	6.3	3	0	3.6
what_other_eviden		6.6	0	21.9	46.9	3.3	0.8	5.8
legal_qual_completed		64.2	45.7	64.4	42.7	66.7	54.9	57.6
legal_qual_attempt		32.9	54.3	32.9	46.9	31.8	42.1	40.4
completed_attempted		0	0	0	0	0	0	0
offence_place		1	0.3	16.4	0	0.4	0	1.1
offence_date		0.2	0	0	0	0.2	0.8	0.2
offence_year		0.2	0	0	0	0.2	0.8	0.2
offence_season		0.2	0	0	0	0.2	0.8	0.2
offence_month		0.2	0	0	0	0.2	0.8	0.2
off_weekday		0.2	0	0	0	0.2	0.8	0.2
off_time		6.6	3.1	1.4	1	5.4	2.3	4.5
off_time_coded		6.6	3.1	1.4	1	5.4	2.3	4.5
hom_start_outdoor		0.4	0	1.4	1	0.2	0	0.3
hom_start_indoor		0.4	0	1.4	1	0.2	0	0.3
hom_finish_outdoor		0.8	45.7	4.1	14.6	3.5	56.4	19.7
hom_finish_indoor		0.8	45.7	4.1	14.6	3.5	56.4	19.7
hom_location_outdoor		0.4	0	1.4	1	0.2	0	0.3
hom_location_indoor		0.4	0	1.4	1	0.2	0	0.3
hom_location		0.4	0	1.4	1	0.2	0	0.3
no_offenders		0	0	0	0	0.4	0	0.1
no_victims		0	0	0	0	0.4	0	0.1
short_decription		0	0	0	0	0	0	0
description_full		0	0	0	0	0	0	0
violence		0	0	0	0	0	0	0
sex_related		0.6	0.7	0	80.2	1.4	1.5	4.7
cruelty		0.6	0.3	0	80.2	1.6	1.5	4.7
affective		10	2.3	6.8	91.7	13.5	20.3	13.2
motive_typology		0	0	0	0	0	0	0
VO_relationship		0.4	0	11	8.3	2.3	0	1.6
VO_relationship_family		0.4	0	11	8.3	2.3	0	1.6
VO_relationship_domestic		0.4	0	11	8.3	2.3	0	1.6
VO_relationship_stranger		0.4	0	11	8.3	2.3	0	1.6
type		0.2	0	0	0	0.2	0	0.1
type_specific		0.2	0	0	0	0.2	0	0.1

BHS Offender Database							
Sample name	Missing data in %						
Variable name	Croatia	Hungary	Kosovo	North Macedonia	Romania	Slovenia	BHS
off_no	0	0	0	0	0	0	0
off_sex	0.4	0	22.3	0	0.1	0	1.1
off_birth	2.5	2.3	20.4	2.8	0.7	1.4	2.7
off_age	2.7	2.1	20.4	2.8	0.3	0.7	2.5
off_age_group	2.7	2.1	20.4	2.8	0.3	0.7	2.5
off_residence	4.4	1.5	47.6	0	0.3	0	3.7
off_nationality	3.2	1.6	26.2	0	0.1	0	2.5
off_ethnicity	4.4	1.8	26.2	0	58.2	0	19.6
off_relationship	4.4	3.6	22.3	0.9	0.9	2.7	3.7
off_marital_status	4.4	3.6	22.3	0.9	0.9	2.7	3.7
off_relationship_status	4.4	3.6	22.3	0.9	0.9	2.7	3.7
off_children	5.7	8.2	28.2	24.3	26.3	0	14
off_children_no	5.7	8.2	28.2	24.3	26.3	0	14
off_education	5.7	10.4	29.1	7.5	8.3	6.2	9.1
off_employ	5	6.3	30.1	8.4	1.5	3.4	5.6
off_income	9.8	7.3	27.2	18.7	4.9	4.1	8.4
off_any_prior_conv	6	6	29.1	1.9	0.6	2.1	5
off_prior_conv	6	6	29.1	1.9	0.6	2.1	5
off_any_viol_prior_conv	7.1	6.6	35.9	5.6	7.1	2.1	7.8
off_viol_prior_conv	7.1	6.6	35.9	5.6	7.1	2.1	7.8
off_prior_prison	7.8	6.6	34	6.5	7.1	2.1	8
off_deten_pretrial	5.9	1.5	32	0.9	2.1	1.4	4
off_deten_pretrial_lenght	9.9	1.5	52.4	15.9	2.8	4.1	7
off_deten_pretrial_lenght_days	9.9	1.5	52.4	15.9	2.8	4.1	7
off_deten_started	10.1	1.6	33	2.8	0	2.1	4.7
off_alt_deten_pretrial	9.4	1.5	47.6	16.8	4.6	3.4	7.2
alt_deten_pretrial_what	9.4	1.2	49.5	16.8	4.9	3.4	7.3
homicide_completed	5	1.5	47.6	5.6	11.5	0	7.4
homicide_attempted	0	0	44.7	29	7.6	0.7	7.5
off_pleas	11.5	6.2	31.1	25.2	2.1	6.2	8.3
expert_psych	8	1.6	33	1.9	1.3	5.5	4.7
off_judged_insane	8.7	1.8	33	3.7	1.3	6.8	5.1
adjudication	7.8	6.7	43.7	0.9	3	5.5	7.2
adjudication_why	10.1	6.9	44.7	7.5	3	5.5	8.1
first_adjudic	1.8	0	8.7	6.5	3.7	2.1	2.3
final_adjudic	3	0.3	20.4	3.7	2.4	1.4	2.7
off_convicted	14.9	4.8	40.8	9.3	4.5	8.2	9.2
procedure_length_days	5.7	0.3	27.2	3.7	2.8	5.5	4.4
procedure_length_months	5.7	0.3	27.2	3.7	2.8	5.5	4.4

BHS Offender Database

Sample name	Missing data in %						
Variable name	Croatia	Hungary	Kosovo	North Macedonia	Romania	Slovenia	BHS
off_beside_hom	0	0	0	0	0	0	0
legal_qualifi_police	6.7	4.8	63.1	2.8	24	0	14.3
legal_qualifi_prosec	8.5	5.6	69.9	1.9	14.3	0.7	11.2
legal_qualifi_first_court	15.8	11.7	66	6.5	14.1	6.2	15.2
legal_qulifi_final	17	8.8	67	10.3	14.3	6.8	14.9
legal_qualifi_police_why	10.8	48.3	63.1	35.5	51.8	39.7	39.7
legal_qualifi_prosec_why	11.5	60.1	72.8	36.4	52.7	38.4	44.2
legal_qualifi_first_court_why	17.6	61.9	68.9	38.3	51.3	39	45.8
legal_qulifi_final_why	18.4	60.5	69.9	38.3	49.9	39	45.2
prison_sent	9.8	1.5	31.1	1.9	2.4	1.4	5.1
long_term_incarceration	9.9	1.5	38.8	0.9	0	1.4	4.7
length_prison	10.6	1.8	29.1	0.9	4.2	1.4	5.6
suspended	18.3	1.5	46.6	12.1	3.4	11	9.4
senten_mitig	20	1.5	50.5	15.9	4.3	12.3	10.3
mitig_circum	30.7	24	58.3	47.7	30.4	28.8	30.4
aggrav_circum	60.6	22.6	78.6	40.2	31.7	19.9	37.6
fine	0	0	0	0	0	0	0
off_intox_alc	22	4.9	35	5.6	1.9	1.4	9.3
off_drugs	28.2	4.5	34	6.5	1.6	2.1	10.7
off_any_addictions	35.6	4.5	34	8.4	10.7	3.4	15.3
off_addiction	35.6	4.5	34	8.4	10.7	3.4	15.3
motive	11	2.1	48.5	2.8	1.9	4.1	6.4
off_weapon	6.7	1.8	32	1.9	1.3	0.7	4.1
gun_license	12.2	2.1	32	32.7	1.5	1.4	7.1
licensed_firearm	6.7	1.8	32	1.9	1.3	0.7	4.1
off_applied	4.4	17.8	32	23.4	6	0.7	10.9
off_suicide	5.7	1.8	32	1.9	1.3	0	3.8
off_suicide_attempt	6.2	1.8	32	1.9	1.3	0	4
off_attempt_commit_suicide	5.5	1.8	32	1.9	1.3	0	3.8
inf_econ	5.3	1.5	39.8	56.1	3	0	7

BHS Victim Database

Sample name Variable name	Missing data in %						
	Croatia	Hungary	Kosovo	North Macedonia	Romania	Slovenia	BHS
vic_no	0	0	0	0	0	0	0
vic_sex	0	0	26	15.5	0.2	0	2.1
vic_birth	15.6	33.7	45.8	53.5	3.7	7.1	21.1
vic_age	4.6	17.4	37.5	24.6	1	5.2	10.3
vic_age_group	4.6	17.4	37.5	24.6	1	5.2	10.3
vic_residence	7.1	0.6	42.7	20.4	0.7	0.6	5.3
vic_nationality	27.2	0.1	28.1	16.9	0.3	0.6	9.5
vic_ethnicity	31.8	0.6	29.2	18.3	57.7	3.2	26.1
vic_marital_status	50.2	20.3	45.8	50.7	4.5	44.5	28.6
vic_children_no	58.1	33.4	52.1	76.1	32	53.5	44.3
vic_education	76.3	71.5	59.4	62.7	10.6	63.2	55.4
vic_employ	49.2	28.3	41.7	51.4	6.4	44.5	31.2
vic_income	66.6	28.5	50	59.9	10.6	50.3	38.1
vic_injury	1.7	0	31.3	18.3	0.3	1.3	3
time_death	1.3	0	29.2	19.7	0	0.6	2.8
vic_public_official	3.1	0	29.2	33.1	0.2	0.6	4.2
vic_public_official_what	4.6	0.4	29.2	38.7	1.8	3.9	5.7
vic_intox_alc	31.6	2	29.2	43.7	0.7	1.3	13.1
off_drugs	39.4	2.7	29.2	44.4	0.5	1.3	29.2
vic_addiction	83.9	2.8	30.2	44.4	8.2	2.6	29.2

Index

© The Author(s) 2021
A.-M. Getoš Kalac, *Violence in the Balkans*, SpringerBriefs in Criminology,
https://doi.org/10.1007/978-3-030-74494-6